Apples, Brie & Chocolate

by Nell Stehr

This book was made possible
with the wonderful help of three dear friends.
Thanks to Charles Mayhew who cleaned up and corrected my spelling and
put commas and periods where they belonged, to Lynne Bergschultz
for her expertise at the drawing board and to Cheryl Gorton
who wore her fingers raw at the computer!

First Edition
ISBN: 0-942495-54-3
Library of Congress Card Number: 96-92170

Published by
Nell Stehr
1672 Sherwood Drive
Cedarburg, Wisconsin 53012

Printed by Palmer Publications, Inc.
P.O. Box 296
Amherst, Wisconsin 54406

Photograph by Don Gilmore

Dedication

*T*o my 95-year-old mother, Freda Lange,
the sweetest mom in the world and
in memory of my loving father, Harold V. Lange

Also to my husband Ken,
my daughter Cynthia and
my sister Wilma.

Oh! Let's include all my relatives and friends!

Renilda (Nell) Lange Stehr spent her childhood in Dubuque, Iowa. During the depression her mother, a superb cook in her own right, took a job outside the home and the young girl's responsibilities escalated, especially in the area of meal preparation. Making dinner often provided Nell with the experience and background necessary for her future as a chef. Her recollections of cooking as a youth: "I made a lot of knopflis."

Marrying Ken Stehr, an avid sportsman and hunter, afforded Nell the opportunity to perfect wild game recipes she would use later in her career. Venison, buffalo, pheasant, partridge, elk, turtle, raccoon and rabbit dishes frequently graced the Stehr's dinner table.

Over the years Nell has amassed over 300 cookbooks. One of her most enjoyable means of relaxation is taking an intriguing cookbook to bed, losing herself in Julia Child the way many of us devour Danielle Steele.

Nell's extracurricular activities seem also to revolve around food, cooking or entertaining. She was a member of the "Cookbook of the Month Club" for twenty years and has prepared feasts too numerous to count for friends, neighbors and family. Riveredge Nature Center has provided Nell with many opportunities to volunteer both in the area of membership development and the culinary arts.

At age 60, when many working people would be dreaming about retirement, the author plunged headlong into a professional career. Her efforts as head chef at the regionally regaled Painted Lady Restaurant in Newburg, Wisconsin, earned accolades like "Perfection" (Carol DeMasters, *Milwaukee Journal*) and "Writing its own history" (Alex Thein, *Milwaukee Sentinel*).

Was it Nell's love of cooking or her burning desire to share with the world years of accumulated culinary experience that drove her to create a cookbook? "Well, not exactly," she exclaims, "I wrote this book just to get people off my back. Period!"

Nell Stehr resides near Cedarburg with her husband Ken, and continues to prepare and cater food for her friends as well as to volunteer at Riveredge Nature Center. As one might expect, her stove never has a chance to cool down.

A

R·e·c·i·p·e·s

*A*nyone who has attempted to choose a title for a book knows how difficult this process can be. Nell's original concept involved a coloring/cookbook combination. So we thought about kids. Kids reminded us of A, B, C's which made us think of samplers – colorful cross-stitch samplers with ornate alphabet letters. So we decided to call the cookbook **The A,B,C's of Nell's Kitchen**. This evolved into **Cooking By The Letter** which became **E Is For Eggplant**. We hope the title, **Apples, Brie & Chocolate** conveys the colorful, sensual, elegant cooking for which Nell Stehr is known.

Charlie   Cheryl   Lynne

Apple and Grape Salad

4 tart unpeeled apples, diced
¾ cup chopped celery
1 cup halved green grapes
⅓ cup coarsely chopped nuts, walnuts
    preferred
1 tablespoon honey
½ cup sour cream
½ cup mayonnaise

Mix the apples, celery, grapes and nuts together. Mix honey, sour cream and mayonnaise. Add to apple mixture, mixing thoroughly.

4 servings

Note…
Can be garnished with thin slices of apple.

Apple-Glazed Cornish Hens

4 Cornish hens, split
salt
pepper
butter
apple jelly, melted

Split Cornish hens in half and arrange in a shallow pan. Salt and pepper both sides, brush with melted butter. Roast at 375º for 30-35 minutes. When they start to brown, brush Cornish hens with hot melted apple jelly two or three times, continuing to roast until tender and golden brown, approximately 15-20 minutes.

4 servings

Au Gratin Onions

2 tablespoons butter
2 tablespoons flour
1 cup milk
2 15-ounce jars canned pearl onions,
    drained, ½ cup liquid reserved
¾ teaspoon salt
¼ teaspoon pepper
1½ cups grated cheese, divided

Melt butter in saucepan. Add flour, stirring for 1 minute. Add milk and reserved liquid from onions and cook until thick. Add salt, pepper, 1 cup of the cheese and onion, stirring to mix. Put into a 2-quart casserole dish. Top with remaining ½ cup cheese. Bake at 400º for 10-15 minutes, just long enough to melt cheese and brown slightly.

4-6 servings

Arroz Con Pollo

4 cups chicken broth
3 whole chicken breasts (6 halves)
1 cup wild rice
1 cup chopped green onion
1 cup chopped celery
6 tablespoons butter, divided
1 cup brown rice
1 teaspoon salt
1 teaspoon thyme
½ teaspoon white pepper
1 pound mushrooms, sliced
1 cup sliced or slivered almonds
1 cup sliced pimento-stuffed green olives

Using enough chicken broth to cover chicken breasts in saucepan, poach chicken until tender, 20-25 minutes. Remove chicken. Reserve broth.

Wash and soak wild rice in warm water for 1 hour. Drain. Sauté onion and celery in 2 tablespoons butter until soft but not browned. Combine wild and brown rice, onion, celery, chicken broth, salt, thyme and white pepper in casserole dish. Cover. Bake at 325° for 45 minutes or until rice is tender. Check three or four times and stir with a fork. If liquid evaporates, add additional chicken stock.

While rice is cooking, slice chicken into strips. In 2 tablespoons of butter, sauté mushrooms. Brown almonds in remaining 2 tablespoons butter.

To serve, arrange chicken, mushrooms, almonds and olives in decorative pattern on top of the rice.

6 servings

Note...
If desired, serve with salsa. Leftover chicken or turkey can be substituted for the fresh chicken.

Apple Squares

5 cups flour
2 tablespoons sugar
½ teaspoon salt
½ teaspoon baking powder
1½ cups shortening
2 egg yolks
water
12 to 15 apples
⅔ cup granulated sugar
⅔ cup brown sugar
1 teaspoon cinnamon
½ teaspoon nutmeg
¼ teaspoon ground cloves
pinch salt
2 tablespoons butter cut in small pieces
cream or milk
sugar

Combine flour, sugar, salt and baking powder; cut in shortening. Beat egg yolks in measuring cup and add enough cold water to make 1 cup. Add to dry ingredients. Mix with a fork, then form into a ball. Divide in half and roll one half to fit a 10x15-inch jelly roll pan. Line pan with dough.

Peel and thinly slice apples. (To keep apples from turning brown, cover with water to which 2 tablespoons lemon juice has been added. Drain.) In a large bowl, combine sugars, cinnamon, nutmeg, cloves and salt with the apples. Spread into the pastry-lined jelly roll pan, and top with pieces of butter.

Roll out remaining dough and place on top of the apples. Cut slits into top crust for steam to escape. Brush top with cream or milk and lightly sprinkle with sugar. Bake at 400° for 50-55 minutes. When cool, drizzle with a thin icing made of confectioners' sugar and milk. Cut into squares.

20 bars

Note...
These can be baked the day before.

Ann's Molasses Thins

Be sure to have plenty of milk on hand for dunking! They'll disappear in no time!

>¾ cup butter
>1 cup sugar
>5 tablespoons dark molasses
>1¾ cups flour
>½ teaspoon salt
>1 teaspoon ginger
>2 teaspoons soda
>1 teaspoon allspice
>sugar for rolling

Cream butter and sugar. Add molasses. Sift together flour, salt, ginger, soda and allspice; add to the butter mixture. Mix thoroughly.

Shape pieces of dough to size no bigger than a marble. Roll in granulated sugar. Press dough flat on buttered cookie sheet with a smooth-bottomed glass which has been greased. Bake at 325º-350º for 8-10 minutes. Leave on cookie sheet to cool.

200 small cookies

Apple Pie Louise

This will become one of your favorite pies, especially at the height of apple season!

Pie Filling
>1½ tablespoons cornstarch
>¾ cup sugar
>¼ teaspoon salt
>1 teaspoon cinnamon
>¼ teaspoon nutmeg
>4 cups peeled and thinly sliced tart apples
>1 tablespoon lemon juice
>1 cup heavy cream
>1 unbaked 9-inch pie crust

Crumb Topping
>½ cup sugar
>½ cup finely crushed graham crackers
>¼ cup flour
>¼ cup chopped walnuts or pecans
>1 tablespoon cinnamon
>⅛ teaspoon nutmeg
>⅓ cup butter, melted

Combine cornstarch, sugar, salt, cinnamon, nutmeg, apples, lemon juice and heavy cream. Blend thoroughly. Turn into pie shell. Bake at 400º for 35 minutes. While baking, assemble the crumb topping.

For topping, combine sugar, graham crackers, flour, nuts, cinnamon and nutmeg. Sprinkle over the top of pie and then spoon the melted butter on top of crumbs. Continue to bake 20-25 minutes longer, or until apples are done and top is golden.

6-8 servings

Almond Layered Cookies

Crust
- 1½ cups graham cracker crumbs
- 1 cup finely chopped almonds (can use walnuts or pecans)
- ½ cup butter
- ¼ cup sugar
- ⅓ cup unsweetened cocoa
- 1 egg, beaten
- 1 teaspoon vanilla

Filling
- ½ cup butter, softened
- 2 tablespoons powdered custard or pudding mix (I use instant chocolate pudding mix.)
- ¼ cup plus 1 tablespoon milk
- 2 cups confectioners' sugar

Topping
- 1½ tablespoons butter
- 4 ounces semi-sweet baking chocolate

Mix crumbs and nuts together. In saucepan, combine butter, sugar, cocoa, eggs and vanilla. Cook and stir over low heat until the consistency of custard, 3-5 minutes. Combine with crumb mixture. Press into a 9x13-inch pan. Place in freezer while preparing next step.

For filling, cream the butter. Blend in pudding mix; blend in milk and slowly add confectioners' sugar. Carefully spread over first layer. Return to freezer.

Over low heat melt butter and chocolate for topping. When combined and melted, carefully spread over second layer. Refrigerate.

When chocolate is set, cut in small squares. Store well-wrapped in refrigerator or freezer until ready to serve.

48 cookies

Success in baking is to have everything at room temperature.

Breakfast Coffee Cake

Batter
 1 cup butter or margarine, softened
 1 cup sugar
 2 eggs
 2 cups flour
 1 teaspoon soda
 1 teaspoon baking powder
 ½ teaspoon salt
 1 cup sour cream
 1 teaspoon almond or vanilla flavoring
 1 16-ounce can cranberry sauce

Icing
 ¾ cup confectioners' sugar
 ¼ teaspoon almond flavoring
 water

Cream butter and sugar; add eggs one at a time, mixing after each addition. In a separate bowl, combine flour, soda, baking powder and salt. Add the dry ingredients to the creamed mixture alternately with sour cream. Add flavoring and mix.

Spread half of the batter in a 7x11-inch glass baking dish. Spread cranberry sauce over the batter. Pour the rest of the batter over the sauce. Bake at 350° for 30-40 minutes or until nicely browned. Let cool 10 minutes.

Combine confectioners' sugar, flavoring and enough water to make a fairly thin icing. Frost. And eat!

8 servings

Note...
For a different flavor, substitute a can of cherry, blueberry or peach pie filling for the cranberry sauce.

Brie in Bread

1 round or oval loaf of white, wheat or rye bread
2 cloves garlic, minced
2 tablespoons butter, melted
1-2 pounds Brie cheese

With a sharp or serrated knife, cut just inside outer edge of bread leaving a shell. Do not cut through bottom. By hand, gently remove the bread and cut it into pieces for dipping. Mix garlic and butter and paint inside of shell with mixture. Reserve remaining butter mixture.

Trim cheese to fit inside shell, leaving rind on if desired. Place loaf on a baking sheet and bake at 350º for 15-20 minutes or until cheese is melted.

Spread the remaining butter mixture on bread pieces. Place on a baking sheet and toast in a 350º oven for 10-15 minutes or until lightly browned. Use to dip in the cheese.

10 servings

Note...
Sliced fruit, such as apples or pears, can also be used for dipping.

Boston Brown Bread

This bread will keep well in the refrigerator or freezer. Excellent served plain with baked beans.

1 cup raisins
1 cup chopped dates
1½ teaspoons soda
3 tablespoons butter
1 cup boiling water
1¾ cups flour
1 cup sugar
½ teaspoon salt
2 eggs
1 teaspoon vanilla
½ cup chopped pecans or walnuts
    (optional)

In a small bowl combine raisins, dates and soda. Add butter; pour boiling water over the mixture. Let stand while you prepare the other ingredients.

Mix flour, sugar and salt. Add fruit mixture, eggs and vanilla and beat well. Add nuts. Divide the batter between two, 1-pound coffee cans that have been well-greased and floured. Bake at 350° for 60-70 minutes or until a toothpick inserted comes out clean. Remove from oven and let sit 5-10 minutes before unmolding.

2 loaves

Note...
This bread is also delicious served with the following spread:
    3-ounce package of cream cheese
    1 small can crushed pineapple, drained.
Mix thoroughly and spread between slices of bread.

Broiled Fish with Herbed Butter

Herbed Butter
    ½ cup (1 stick) butter, softened
    1 tablespoon chopped parsley
    few drops of lemon juice
    salt and pepper to taste
    1 tablespoon of any of following herbs
        or combination: basil, thyme, oregano,
        chives
Marinade
    ½ cup oil
    ¼ cup lemon juice
    4 drops Worcestershire sauce
    salt and pepper
Fish
    4 8-ounce fish filets - sole, scrod,
        roughy, cod, trout or whatever fish
        you care to use

Mix butter, parsley, lemon juice, salt and pepper and herbs well. Reshape butter into original shape and chill. Cut into squares.

For marinade, mix oil, lemon juice, Worcestershire sauce, salt and pepper together.

Arrange fish on well-oiled broiler pan. Broil 4-6 minutes on each side, basting twice with the marinade.

Serve fish hot with a square of herbed butter and slice of lemon on each filet.

4 servings

Note...
Any extra butter can be frozen for future use.

Beef Wellington

Pâté

    1 pound mushrooms
    1 bunch green onions
    ⅓ pound Canadian bacon or ham
    3 tablespoons butter
    ¼ teaspoon garlic powder
    ¾ teaspoon salt
    ½ teaspoon ground pepper

Madeira Sauce

    4 tablespoons butter
    4 tablespoons minced green onion
    1 cup water
    1 teaspoon beef base
    ½ cup Madeira wine

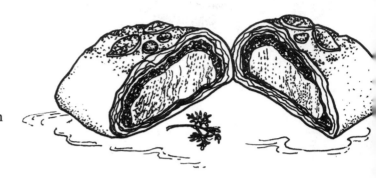

    3-4 pounds whole tenderloin, trimmed and at room temperature
    1 17¼-ounce package frozen puff pastry, thawed
    1 egg, beaten

In a food processor with steel blade, coarsely chop the mushrooms, green onions, Canadian bacon or ham for the pâté; sauté in butter until liquid is almost all evaporated. Add the garlic powder, salt and pepper. Cool.

Sauté the tenderloin quickly in large, hot skillet, browning all sides. Cool. Reserve pan juices.

Melt butter for the sauce; add reserved pan juices and onions. Simmer slowly for 5 minutes; do not brown onions. Dissolve beef base in water. Add beef base solution and wine to sauce. Simmer 5 minutes.

Place tenderloin on pastry; top with pâté. Wrap tenderloin in pastry and seal, trimming edges as needed. Place Wellington seam-side down on a 10½ x 15-inch jelly roll pan which has been sprayed with vegetable spray. Adorn top with leftover pastry that has been cut into decorative shapes. Cover and refrigerate for 2 hours.

Preheat oven to 375°. Brush Wellington with beaten egg. For medium rare, bake 25-30 minutes, until pastry is nicely browned. Cool 5-10 minutes before cutting. To serve, spoon 1-2 tablespoons of Madeira Sauce on dinner plate; add a slice of Wellington; garnish with parsley or watercress. The remaining Madeira Sauce may be served on the side.

6-8 servings

Cynthia's Favorite Chicken

3 large chicken breasts, boned and cut in
   half
salt and pepper
¼ cup butter or oil
8 fresh mushrooms, sliced or 1 7-ounce
   can mushrooms
1 10¾-ounce can cream of mushroom
   soup
1 10¾-ounce can cream of chicken soup
1 5-ounce can sliced water chestnuts,
   drained
2 tablespoons chopped green pepper
2 tablespoons finely chopped celery
¼ teaspoon thyme
¼ cup white wine (optional)

L ightly season chicken with salt and
pepper and brown slowly in butter
or oil. Save drippings. Arrange chicken
in 7x11-inch glass baking dish. Add
mushrooms to drippings and sauté a
few minutes. Then add soups and stir
until smooth. Add water chestnuts,
green pepper, celery, thyme and wine.
Heat to boiling; pour over the chicken.
Cover and bake at 350º for 25 minutes.
Uncover and continue to bake for 20
minutes more or until chicken is
tender.

4-6 servings

Note…
*You can use legs and thighs or a whole
chicken cut up in place of the chicken
breasts.*

*Gourmet Wild Rice on page 33 is a great
addition to this dish!*

R•e•c•i•p•e•s

Crab or Shrimp Appetizer

2 6½-ounce cans of crab (or 1 pound
   shrimp, cleaned and cut in small
   pieces)
1 teaspoon minced onion
1 teaspoon minced celery
1 teaspoon minced green pepper
2 teaspoons lemon juice
½ teaspoon grated lemon rind
¼ teaspoon salt
4-5 drops Tabasco
dash pepper
¼ cup mayonnaise

Mix shrimp, onion, celery, green pepper, lemon juice, lemon rind, salt, Tabasco, pepper and mayonnaise together and chill. Serve on buttered rounds or squares of bread, or on crackers.

30-40 appetizers

Cranberry Salad

1 pound cranberries
2 apples, peeled and cored
½ pound marshmallows
1 cup sugar
1 cup cream, whipped

Grind cranberries and apples in food processor. Cut the marshmallows into small pieces; combine cranberries, apples, marshmallows and sugar. Let stand overnight. Add the whipped cream before serving.

8 servings

Note…
For a special presentation use individual salad plates upon which individual lettuce leaves have been placed. Cover with rings of sliced pineapple followed by scoops of cranberry salad. Top with green maraschino cherries.

By the Author

Caesar Salad

1 egg
1 head romaine lettuce
½ cup parmesan cheese, grated
1 egg
Dressing
½ cup olive oil
2 tablespoons wine vinegar
⅓ teaspoon salt
¼ teaspoon mustard
1 clove garlic, minced
¾ teaspoon Worcestershire sauce
fresh ground pepper
Garlic Croutons
3 tablespoons butter, softened
4 slices French bread
½ teaspoon garlic powder

Coddle egg by placing enough water to cover the egg in a saucepan; bring to a boil. Drop egg into the water and let stand 1 minute. Remove egg; cool.

Make dressing in a mixing bowl by combining olive oil, vinegar, salt, mustard, garlic, Worcestershire sauce and pepper. Mix well.

For croutons, spread butter over both sides of bread and sprinkle with garlic powder. Cut into ½-inch cubes. Place on baking sheet and bake at 350° for 15 minutes or until they are crisp and dry.

Clean lettuce, removing the hard core. Add the beaten coddled egg and enough salad dressing to coat. Toss. Top with croutons. Garnish with fresh, grated Parmesan cheese.

4 servings

Note…
For a main course salad add lightly-seasoned chicken or beef tenderloin strips sautéed in butter. Yum! Any extra dressing will keep refrigerated for several days.

Chicken Noodle Soup

Take a serving of this to a sick friend. It will help the healing process!

2 medium onions
5 large carrots
5 ribs celery, including leaves
1 chicken, 4-5 pounds
3 quarts water
2 tablespoons chicken base (preferred) or 4 bouillon cubes
½ pound noodles, handmade or store-bought

Quarter 1 onion and chunk 2 carrots. Combine in large stock pot with 2 whole ribs celery, chicken, water and chicken base. Simmer 45 minutes to 1 hour or until chicken is tender. Remove chicken and vegetables from broth. Strain broth through a clean towel or cheesecloth, reserving broth. Discard vegetables.

Chop remaining onion, slice carrots and cut celery into small pieces, discarding leaves. Add to broth and return to stove. Cook until tender. Meanwhile bone and cut chicken into bite-sized pieces. Cook noodles in salted water. When the vegetables are cooked, add the cooked noodles and cut chicken. Adjust seasonings. Bring back to boil. Serve. Garnish with chopped fresh or dried parsley.

4-5 servings as a main course, or 8 as a first course

Note…
Wonderful served with Lavosh Crackers, recipe on page 57.

Chicken Imperial

2 cups bread crumbs
¼ cup minced parsley
1 clove garlic, minced
1½ teaspoons salt
⅛ teaspoon pepper
1 cup butter, melted
1 tablespoon Dijon mustard
1 teaspoon Worcestershire sauce
8 whole chicken breasts, boned and halved

Combine bread crumbs, parsley, garlic, salt and pepper in a shallow bowl. Mix together melted butter, mustard and Worcestershire sauce. Dip each piece of chicken into the butter mixture then into crumbs, making sure to coat thoroughly. Arrange chicken pieces in shallow baking pan in one layer. Sprinkle any remaining butter mixture over top. Bake, uncovered, at 350° for about 1 hour or until juices run clear.

8 servings (or 16 half-breast servings)

Crème Caramel

1½ cups sugar, divided
½ cup water
6 eggs
2¾ cups milk, scalded

In a saucepan combine 1 cup of the sugar and water. Bring to a boil; cover and cook rapidly until golden brown. Quickly pour into 6 glass custard cups. Set aside.

Beat eggs with remaining ½ cup sugar until well blended; add milk slowly, beating all the while. Skim bubbles from top and pour mixture through a fine sieve into custard cups. Set cups into a shallow pan and fill with hot water half the way up the sides of cups. Bake at 350° for 20 minutes or until set. Cool.

To serve, run a knife around the edge of each cup and unmold onto serving plate. Can be garnished with whipped cream and a strawberry.

6 servings

Chocolate Walnut Pie

1 unbaked 9-inch shell
3 ounces semi-sweet chocolate, melted
4 eggs
1 cup brown sugar
1 cup corn syrup, light or dark
½ cup butter, melted
1 teaspoon vanilla
¼ teaspoon salt
1 cup chopped walnuts
1 cup whipping cream

Spread the bottom of pie shell with melted chocolate. Refrigerate until chocolate sets. Meanwhile, beat eggs. Add sugar, syrup, butter, vanilla, salt and walnuts. Pour into chilled pie crust. Bake at 350° for 40-50 minutes or until set.

Serve with whipped cream and top with shaved chocolate curls.

6-8 servings

Note...
To make curls, shave a chocolate candy bar with a potato peeler.

Cornucopia with Fruit

Cornucopia
> 2 eggs
> ⅔ cup sugar
> 1 teaspoon lemon juice
> ¼ teaspoon salt
> ⅔ cup sifted flour
> 2 tablespoons butter, melted

Vanilla Sauce
> 2 cups half-and-half
> ½ vanilla bean split or 1 teaspoon pure vanilla extract
> 2 eggs
> ½ cup sugar
> fresh fruit such as raspberries, strawberries, blueberries, peaches, pears or crushed bananas

B eat eggs; gradually add sugar. Beat well for 3 minutes. Blend in lemon juice, salt and flour. Stir in butter; mix well.

Trace 8 6-inch circles on parchment paper. Turn paper over so the pencil mark doesn't come in contact with the batter. Spray each circle lightly with vegetable spray. Put 2 tablespoons of batter on each circle and spread to the edge of the circle. Bake at 350º until lightly browned, 4-5 minutes.

Remove at once. Working very quickly, shape each circle into a cone. Put into a glass to keep from unrolling. If they become brittle, return cones to the oven to soften, or eat them!

For sauce, combine half-and-half and vanilla in saucepan, bring just to the boiling point. In a bowl, whisk eggs and sugar, combining well. Add to the hot mixture in a slow stream, stirring well. Cook mixture over low heat, stirring constantly, until slightly thickened. Do not let it boil. To be safe, use a candy thermometer and remove pan from heat when mixture reaches 175º. Strain sauce through a fine sieve, and return to pan. Cool saucepan by floating it in ice water, continually stirring sauce. Cover and refrigerate until cold. This sauce will keep for 2 days.

Place a tablespoon or two of the sauce in narrow glasses (champagne glasses work well). Add cornucopia, then add fresh fruit and more custard. Top with fruit and a sprig of mint.

8 servings

Note…
For a simpler version, use a commercial "sugar cone" instead of the cornucopia.

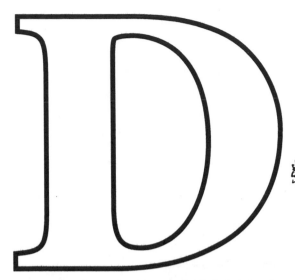

D

R·e·c·i·p·e·s

Margarita Punch

3 cups tequila
2 cups triple sec
1 cup fresh lime juice
2 quarts club soda, chilled
ice ring containing lime slices
lime wedges
coarse salt

Combine tequila, triple sec and lime juice. Refrigerate until ready to serve. Add club soda and ice ring. Run a wedge of lime around glasses and dip rims in coarse salt. Fill with punch.

24 4-ounce cups

Citrus Cooler

4 cups water, divided
¼ cup sugar
3 cups pineapple juice
1 6-ounce can frozen orange juice
   concentrate
½ cup lemon juice
3 12-ounce cans lemon-lime soda,
   chilled
1½ cups vodka or to taste (optional)
10-12 ice cubes or ice ring containing
   lemon slices

Combine sugar and 1 cup water. Heat, stirring until sugar is dissolved. Cool. Mix with pineapple juice, remaining water, orange juice and lemon juice. Chill. Just before serving, stir in soda and vodka; add ice cubes or ice ring.

20-24 5-ounce servings

Cranberry Punch

2 12-ounce cans orange juice
   concentrate
2 12-ounce cans frozen lemonade
   concentrate
1 46-ounce jar cranberry juice
1 liter ginger ale or 7-Up
1 cup vodka (optional)

Combine orange juice, lemonade and cranberry juice. Refrigerate until ready to use. At serving time add ginger ale and vodka.

Make ice ring of additional cranberry juice, so as not to dilute the punch.

20-25 5-ounce glasses

Champagne Punch

1 cup sugar
1 48-ounce can pineapple juice
1 cup lemon juice
1 6-ounce can frozen orange juice
   concentrate
1 750 ML bottle white wine (Rhine or
   Chablis)
2 750 ML bottles champagne
ice ring containing orange slices and
   maraschino cherries

Combine sugar and pineapple, lemon and orange juices, mixing well to dissolve sugar. Chill for several hours.

Make an ice ring with orange slices and maraschino cherries.

Before serving, place ice ring in punch bowl. Pour in sugar and juice mixture. Add wine and champagne. Garnish with additional orange slices. Serve at once.

35 5-ounce servings

Sparkling white grape juice and non-alcoholic wines can be used to make this an alcohol-free punch.

Bloody Mary Punch

4 quarts tomato juice, chilled
1 pint vodka, chilled
Worcestershire sauce
Tabasco sauce
celery salt
pickle sticks
celery sticks
ice cubes made from tomato juice (so
  they do not dilute the punch)

Mix tomato juice and vodka. You can add the Worcestershire sauce and Tabasco to taste, but I prefer to have them on the side, along with celery salt, pickle sticks, celery sticks and ice cubes, to let everyone add to their own taste. Garnish punch with thin slices of lemon.

24 6-ounce cups

Note...
Spark up your Blood Mary with a Dilly Bean, page 19, or a spear of pickled asparagus.

Snow Shoe Drink

1 part brandy
1 part Peppermint Schnapps

Combine and serve over cracked ice.

Dilly Beans

2 pounds green or yellow beans,
  trimmed
1 teaspoon cayenne pepper, divided
  (optional)
4 heads fresh dillweed, divided, or
  4 tablespoons dill seed
2½ cups water
2½ cups vinegar
¼ cup canning salt

Pack beans lengthwise into 4 sterilized pint-jars, leaving ¼ inch of space on top. To each jar, add ¼ teaspoon cayenne and 1 head dillweed or 1 tablespoon dill seed. Meanwhile, in small saucepan, boil the water, vinegar and salt to make brine. Pour boiling brine over beans. Adjust caps. Process pints 10 minutes in boiling water bath.

4 pints

Dressing

This dressing goes well as a side dish for chicken or fish.

2 cups bread cubes
1 cup chicken or vegetable broth
¼ cup butter
1 cup mushrooms, sliced
2 onions, chopped
¼ cup shredded carrots
1 egg
1 clove garlic, minced
½ cup chopped parsley
1½ teaspoons salt
¼ teaspoon pepper
1½ tablespoons lemon juice
2 tablespoons butter

Soften bread cubes in broth. Melt butter and sauté mushrooms, onions and carrots until soft. Beat egg slightly and add to bread, then add garlic, parsley, salt, pepper, lemon juice and sautéed vegetables. Mix. Place in a 1½-quart casserole dish and top with small pieces of butter. Bake at 350° for 20-30 minutes or until heated through. Recipe can be doubled.

4 servings

they're at it again !!!

Roast Duck

2 carrots, cut up
1 stalk celery
1 small onion
1 large duck, cleaned and cut in half
one or more of the following herbs:
    rosemary, poultry seasoning, thyme
soy sauce

Currant Sauce
½ cup red wine
½ cup orange juice
1 cup chicken broth
¼ cup lemon juice
¾ cup currant jelly
⅛ teaspoon ground ginger
pinch cayenne pepper
¼ teaspoon salt
¼ cup cornstarch
¼ cup water

In a roasting pan combine carrots, celery and onion with a small amount of water. Cover with a baking rack. Season the cavity of the duck with a selection of herbs. Place duck on rack and rub with soy sauce. Cover with foil; roast at 350° for 2-2 ½ hours or until tender. Remove foil the last 30 minutes to crisp duck.

To make sauce, combine wine, orange juice, chicken broth, lemon juice, currant jelly, ground ginger, pepper and salt. Bring to a boil. Mix cornstarch with water. Add to wine mixture and boil for 4-5 minutes. If too thick, add more chicken broth to thin. Serve with roast duck.

4 servings

"Wild" Dinner Party Invitation by the Author

E

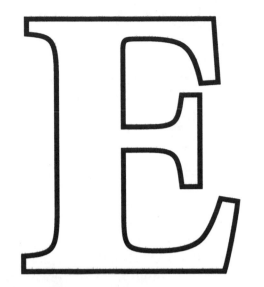

Eggplant Adliner

3 tablespoons oil
1 green pepper, julienned
1 medium onion, sliced
2 cups sliced zucchini, cut in ⅛ inch
    slices
2 cups sliced, fresh mushrooms
3 cups cubed eggplant
3 cloves garlic, crushed
1 teaspoon salt
½ teaspoon pepper
2 teaspoons fresh or 1½ teaspoons dried
    basil
1 28-ounce can stewed tomatoes
1 15-ounce can tomato sauce
6 ounces cashew nuts or sunflower seeds
    (optional)
6 ounces Parmesan cheese, shredded
6 ounces American cheese, shredded

In a large skillet or Dutch oven, heat oil. Add green pepper, onion and zucchini; sauté lightly. Add mushrooms, eggplant, garlic, salt, pepper and basil. Sauté for 6-8 minutes, then add tomatoes and tomato sauce. Continue to cook for 8 minutes. Put contents into a 2½-quart casserole or 6 individual ramekins. Add cashews and lightly stir. Top first with Parmesan cheese, then the American cheese. Bake at 350° for 20-30 minutes until warmed through and cheese is melted and lightly browned.

6 servings

Note...
Add a gourmet touch by sautéing thinly sliced medallions of veal in a small amount of butter until browned. Add it to the other ingredients prior to baking. Yummy!

Egg Nog

6 eggs, separated
¾ cup sugar
1 pint brandy or whiskey
¾ cup milk
½ pint half and half
½ pint heavy cream
nutmeg

Beat egg yolks with sugar and brandy. Add milk and light cream. Beat egg whites to soft peak. Whip heavy cream until fluffy. Fold both into yolk mixture. Chill. Serve with sprinkled nutmeg.

2 quarts

Elaine's King Crab Pâté

1   12-ounce package frozen crab meat, thawed
½ cup butter, softened
2 tablespoons lemon juice
3 hard-cooked eggs
½ cup mayonnaise
⅓ cup grated Parmesan cheese
1½ teaspoons horseradish
½ teaspoon salt
¼ teaspoon garlic powder
white pepper
¼ cup minced onion
¼ cup chopped parsley

Drain and slice crab. Whip butter and lemon juice until light and fluffy.

Slice eggs in half and remove yolks, reserving whites. Chop yolks and beat into butter mixture with mayonnaise, Parmesan cheese, horseradish, salt, garlic powder and pepper.

Finely chop egg whites and add with crab, onion and parsley to butter mixture. Pack into small serving bowl. Chill several hours.

3 cups

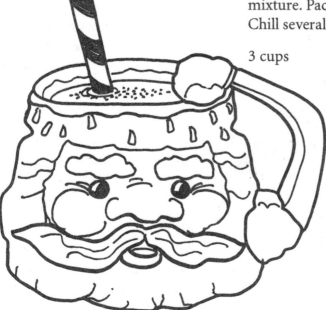

Eddie Wilger's Torte

1 pound butter, softened
2 cups sugar, divided
12 eggs, separated
4 cups cake flour
1 cup cocoa
½ teaspoon salt
⅓ cup cream
1 teaspoon vanilla

Custard Filling
2 cups cream (or half-and-half)
6 egg yolks
½ cup flour
¼ teaspoon salt
1 cup butter, softened
1 teaspoon vanilla (or 2 tablespoons of
   your favorite liquor)

Easy Chocolate Frosting
1 cup whipping cream
12 ounces semi-sweet chocolate, shaved

Cream butter; gradually add 1 cup sugar. One at a time, add egg yolks, beating after each addition. Sift flour, cocoa and salt and add to butter mixture. Add cream and mix well.

Beat egg whites until stiff but not dry. Slowly add the remaining cup of sugar and beat until soft peaks form. Fold egg whites into the above mixture. Add vanilla.

Preheat oven to 350°. Place parchment paper on a cookie sheet and, with an 8-inch cake pan, draw circles. Reverse paper so pencil marks are not near the batter and place 4-5 tablespoons of the batter in each circle, spreading evenly to fill circle. Bake 5-10 minutes, just until edges start to turn brown. Remove layers from pan and place between sheets of parchment paper or waxed paper until all layers are baked. There should be 14-15 layers.

For Custard Filling, combine cream, egg yolks, flour and salt in double boiler; cook until thick. Remove. Add butter, a small amount at a time, beating until creamy. Add vanilla. Set aside until cold.

For Easy Chocolate Frosting, in double boiler, heat cream until boiling. Add chocolate and stir until chocolate is melted and smooth. Cool until spreading consistency.

Spread filling between all layers but not on top layer. You may need to use toothpicks to hold layers and keep them from sliding. If cake layers seem uneven, trim layers to make even and round. Frost with chocolate frosting and refrigerate. Remove 10 minutes before serving.

14 servings

Eddie, one of our regular customers at the Painted lady, would always inquire if this particular torte was available before he ordered dinner. We always tried to please our customers!

Egg Nog Pie

Crust
>1½ cups graham cracker crumbs
>⅓ cup butter, melted
>2 tablespoons sugar
>½ cup finely chopped almonds
>   (optional)

Filling
>¼ cup cold water
>1 tablespoon gelatin
>4 large eggs, separated
>¼ teaspoon salt
>1 cup sugar, divided
>½ cup milk
>1½ tablespoons rum
>whipped cream
>nutmeg

Combine graham cracker crumbs, butter, sugar and almonds; press into a 9-inch pie pan. Bake at 350º for 8 minutes. Cool.

In cold water, soften gelatin. Set aside. In a double boiler heat egg yolks until light and lemon colored. Add salt, ½ cup sugar and milk. Heat, stirring constantly until mixture coats a metal spoon. Add gelatin and continue to cook until gelatin is dissolved. Cool custard.

Beat egg whites until soft peaks form, then gradually add remaining ½ cup sugar and continue to beat until stiff peaks form. Fold whites and rum into custard. Pour into crust and refrigerate until set.

Garnish with whipped cream and sprinkle with nutmeg.

6 servings

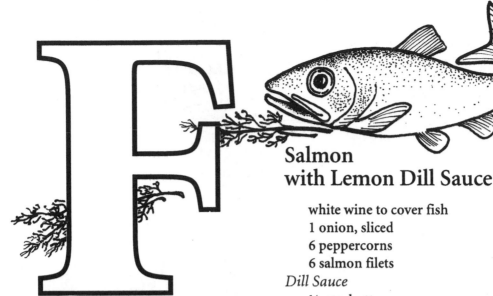

Salmon with Lemon Dill Sauce

white wine to cover fish
1 onion, sliced
6 peppercorns
6 salmon filets

Dill Sauce
  ½ cup butter
  ¼ cup flour
  2 cups canned clam juice
  ⅓ cup fresh lemon juice
  1 tablespoon dried dill (or 2 tablespoons
    fresh dill)
  salt and pepper to taste
  green onions, finely chopped

Heat wine, onion and peppercorns in large skillet and add salmon filets. Poach on low heat for 7-10 minutes depending on thickness of filets, or until done. Test to see if fish flakes.

Melt butter over low heat; add flour and cook for 2½-3 minutes. Add clam juice and bring back to a boil, stirring constantly until thick and creamy. Add lemon juice, dill, salt and pepper. Remove salmon from poaching liquid, discarding liquid, onion and peppercorns. Place filets on serving dish; add small amount of sauce around the fish. Garnish with finely chopped green onions. Serve remaining sauce on the side.

6 servings

Filet of Sole Cardinal

2 slices bread, cubed
water
3 green onions, chopped
1 stalk celery, chopped
2 tablespoons butter
1¼ teaspoon Paul Prudhomme's
    Seafood Magic Spice, divided
2 cups stewed tomatoes
1 clove garlic
4 mushrooms, sliced
8 4-ounce filets of sole
butter, room temperature
paprika
½ cup wine (optional)

Soften bread in a small amount of water. Squeeze out excess moisture. Set aside. Sauté onion and celery in butter. Add to bread along with ¾ teaspoon Seafood Magic seasoning. Set aside.

For sauce, grind tomatoes, garlic, remaining ½ teaspoon Seafood Magic and mushrooms with butter in a food processor. Heat in a small saucepan and simmer for 15 minutes. Set aside.

In a 7x9-inch baking dish lay 4 pieces of sole. Spread bread mixture over filets, cover with remaining filets. Spread with soft butter, dust with paprika. Sprinkle with ½ cup wine. Bake at 375° for 15-20 minutes or until fish flakes. Serve with re-heated red sauce.

4 servings

Baby Coho Salmon, Shrimp-Stuffed

4 baby salmon, cleaned but left whole
12 shrimp, cleaned
4 tablespoons butter, divided
1 stalk celery, chopped
1½ small onions, chopped
3 slices bread, cubed
water or chicken broth
salt and pepper to taste
¼ cup butter, melted
paprika

Remove heads (optional) and wash fish well. Sauté cleaned shrimp in 2 tablespoons of butter. Set aside. In remaining 2 tablespoons of butter, sauté celery and onion until tender but not brown. Soften bread in a small amount of water or chicken broth. Squeeze out excess moisture. Combine bread, shrimp and celery and onion mixture; salt and pepper to taste.

Open the fish and spread bread mixture on one side of the fish. Top with 3 shrimp. Cover with other side of fish. Brush with melted butter, sprinkle with paprika. Bake at 400° for 20-25 minutes or until browned and cooked through.

4 servings

Note...
If you're lucky enough to live in the Milwaukee area, a great place for fresh fish is the Empire Fish Co.

Cod En Papillotte

6 ounces mushrooms, sliced
2 tablespoons olive oil
2 tablespoons butter
1 bunch green onions, chopped
   (save some green tops)
salt and pepper to taste
½ cup mayonnaise
½ teaspoon dry mustard
2 teaspoons dill weed
4-8 cod filets
2 tomatoes, sliced
4 thin slices lemon

Cut parchment paper into four 12 x12-inch pieces. Fold each square in half and cut into a heart shape. Set aside.

In saucepan, sauté mushrooms in oil and butter. Add onions, salt and pepper. Cool.

Mix mayonnaise, mustard and dill weed together. Set aside.

Unfold parchment hearts and place fish on one side of each heart. Top filets with mushroom mixture and 2 tomato slices. Spread with mayonnaise mixture and top with lemon slice. Fold parchment over fish and pleat edges tightly. Bake at 400° for 20 minutes or until paper is puffed and light brown.

With shears or sharp knife, cut opening in top of parchment, folding paper back to expose fish. Serve on dinner plate. Garnish with a slice of lemon and reserved green onion tops.

4 servings

Note...
This dish works equally well with sole, salmon, pike or red snapper.

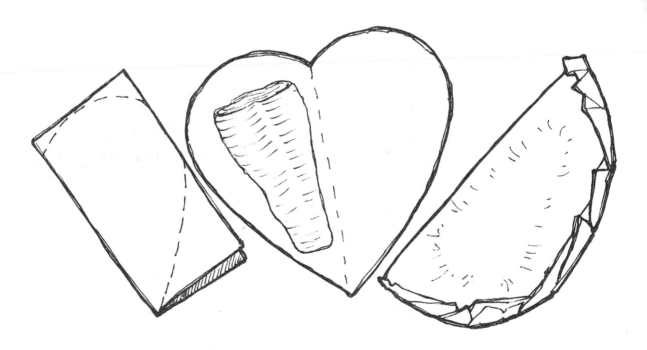

Fettuccine Alfredo

Fettuccine
- 2¼ cups flour
- 3 eggs
- 1 teaspoon salt
- 3 tablespoons water
- 1 tablespoon oil

Alfredo Sauce
- ½ cup (1 stick butter), softened
- 1 egg yolk
- ¼ cup whipping cream
- ½ cup freshly grated Parmesan cheese

Mix flour, eggs, salt, water and oil together and knead for 5-10 minutes until a soft, but not sticky, dough is formed. Let rest, covered, for ½ hour. Divide dough in half and roll out to ⅛-inch thickness. Cut in four pieces, stack evenly, and cut into ¼-inch strips. Flour generously to prevent sticking. Repeat procedure with other half of dough.

Bring a large kettle of slightly salted water to boil. While stirring constantly, gently add noodles. When water returns to the boiling point, cook the noodles for 2-3 more minutes or until tender. Drain and rinse thoroughly in cold water. If you prepare the fettuccine ahead of time, lightly oil and refrigerate.

Prepare the Alfredo Sauce by beating butter, egg yolk, whipping cream and Parmesan cheese together.

Place the Alfredo sauce and fettuccine in a medium-sized saucepan and stir over very low heat until heated through. You may have to add small amount of cream or half and half to achieve a smooth, not too thick, sauce.

4-6 servings

Fondu Chocolat

- 9 ounces Toblenene (or any semi-sweet chocolate) chocolate, broken in pieces
- ½ cup heavy cream
- 2 tablespoons Cointreau or Grand Marnier liqueur

Combine chocolate, cream and Cointreau or Grand Marnier in a quart saucepan. Stir over very low heat until chocolate is melted and mixture is smooth. Keep warm in chafing dish over a candle.

For dunking use long pieces of sponge cake, lady fingers, apple wedges or other fruits.

1½ cups

Note...
Use the Fondu Chocolat for a base under slices of cheesecake, shortcakes or tortes. Also just great over ice cream!

Frozen Pumpkin Delicacy

Pecan Crumb Crust
>1 cup fine graham cracker crumbs (12-14 squares)
>½ cup finely chopped pecans
>¼ teaspoon salt
>¼ cup butter, softened
>1 tablespoon honey

Filling
>1¾ cups pumpkin, cooked or canned
>½ teaspoon salt
>½ teaspoon ground nutmeg
>½ teaspoon ground ginger
>½ teaspoon ground cinnamon
>1 cup honey
>1 envelope (¼ ounce) unflavored gelatin
>1 cup whipping cream, whipped
>2 cups vanilla ice cream, softened slightly
>toasted pecans (optional)

In bowl combine graham cracker crumbs, pecans, salt, butter and honey. Press into 9- or 10-inch pie plate. Bake at 375° for 5-7 minutes or until lightly browned. Cool crust.

In saucepan combine pumpkin, salt, nutmeg, ginger, cinnamon, honey and gelatin. Cook over low heat, stirring constantly until gelatin is dissolved, about 5 minutes. Chill until mixture is cooled and starting to set, 1-1¼ hours. Fold in whipped cream.

To assemble, spread ice cream over chilled crust. Spread pumpkin mixture over ice cream. (Mixture will mound high in 9-inch pie plate.) Arrange toasted pecan halves on top of pie in attractive spoke-like arrangement, if desired.

Place pie unwrapped in freezer. When solidly frozen (after about 2 hours), cover with plastic wrap and/or aluminum foil and return to freezer. Remove 10-15 minutes before serving.

8 servings

Note...
To toast pecan halves, combine with 1 tablespoon melted butter, spread on baking sheet and toast in 350° oven 5 minutes. Sprinkle lightly with salt. Cool.

Family's Favorite Cheesecake

1 cup vanilla wafer or graham cracker crumbs
6 tablespoons butter, melted
2½ pounds cream cheese, room temperature
1¾ cups sugar
½ cup sour cream
5 eggs
2 teaspoons vanilla

Mix together cookie crumbs and butter and press into the bottom of a 10-inch springform pan.

With electric mixer or processor with steel blade, beat cheese until light and fluffy. Add sugar slowly, then sour cream. Blend. Add eggs, one at a time; blend. Add vanilla and blend. Turn into pan and bake at 300° for 1 hour or until mixture is set. Turn oven off and let rest in oven for 1 hour more.

Variations

Change the crust by adding ½ cup finely chopped pecans, almonds or walnuts, or use chocolate cookie crumbs or Oreo Cookies.

Add 3 squares of unsweetened chocolate, melted, for a chocolate cheesecake.

Instead of the vanilla, substitute any liquor such as ¼ cup Kaluha, Tia Maria, Irish Cream, etc.

Coarsely chop two of any candy bars, such as English Toffee, Butter Fingers, Peanut Butter Cups, peppermint candy, and add it to the filling - use your imagination.

Frost with the Easy Chocolate Frosting from Eddie Wilger's Torte on page 23 and garnish with nuts or cherries.

Have fun!

12-16 servings

G

Garniture

In cooking it is a well-known fact that discriminating diners "eat" with their eyes, as well as their palates.

Garnishes can add a much-needed something to otherwise bland or boring looking meals. Nell tries to balance warm colors (the orange of carrots, tomatoes or shrimp) with the cool colors (the greens of pea pods, parsley, broccoli, tops of green onions or dill). Nothing breaks the monotony of the surface of a crock of tomato bisque like a few, well-placed croutons or a sprig of emerald-green parsley. If your salad bores you to tears, serve it on a bed of purple kale or top it off with a few violet or nasturtium flowers for some added visual punch as well as flavor.

Don't forget dessert garnishes! Colorful fruit (strawberries, raspberries, cherries, blueberries, kiwi, star fruit, a sprig of mint, thin orange slices, lemons or lime) or a sprinkling of chopped nuts not only enhance the appearance but also the flavor of everything from puddings to parfaits.

R·e·c·i·p·e·s

Garlic Individual Strata

    7 cloves garlic, crushed
    2 cups milk
    4 eggs
    1 scant teaspoon salt
    ¼ teaspoon pepper
    4 tablespoons minced parsley
    1 tablespoon onion, finely chopped
    1 loaf cubed French or Italian bread

Bring garlic and milk to a boil. Remove from heat and let sit for 15-20 minutes. Meanwhile, lightly beat eggs with salt and pepper. Strain milk through a fine sieve into beaten eggs. Discard garlic. Stir in parsley and onion.

Generously butter 6 large cups of a muffin tin. Fill cups with cubed bread. Pour the egg mixture over the cubes. Let rest for 15-20 minutes. (Can be set aside at this point for up to 4 hours, refrigerated.) Bake at 350° for 40-45 minutes or until puffed and browned. Wait a few minutes before unmolding.

6 servings

Note…
Muffins will shrink a bit. Any leftover cubes of bread can be used for croutons. Recipe under Caesar Salad, page 13.

Gazpacho

    1 medium cucumber, cut in small pieces
    2 pounds tomatoes, peeled, seeded and
        chopped
    1 red bell pepper, julienned
    1 yellow pepper, julienned
    1 cup finely chopped red onion
    1 teaspoon minced garlic
    ¼ cup olive oil
    ¼ cup red wine vinegar
    1 cup tomato juice
    1 teaspoon cumin
    1 teaspoon salt
    1 tablespoon Worcestershire sauce
    1 tablespoon tomato paste

Mix all ingredients. Chill 2 - 3 hours before serving. Serve in soup bowls, garnished with thin slices of cucumber.

6-8 servings

Gourmet Wild Rice

1¼ cups wild rice
water
⅓ cup butter
½ cup chopped green onion (including
   tops)
1 cup diagonally sliced celery
½ cup chopped parsley
½ pound mushrooms, sliced
2½ cups chicken broth
1 teaspoon salt
1 teaspoon thyme

Wash rice well; cover with water and let stand for at least an hour. Drain thoroughly. Melt butter and lightly sauté green onions, celery, parsley and mushrooms. In a covered baking dish combine the rice, chicken broth, salt and thyme. Stir in the sautéed ingredients. Cover and bake at a 325º for 45 minutes or until tender and the liquid is all absorbed.

8-10 servings

Note…
This dish reheats very well. Add more chicken broth if it seems dry.

Rice packed in custard cups then inverted on dinner plates or around the edge of a platter of meat makes an eye-catching presentation.

Grand Old-Fashioned Cheesecake Squares

Graham Cracker Crust
    1½ cups graham cracker crumbs
    ¼ cup sugar
    ¼ cup chopped almonds (optional)
    ½ teaspoon cinnamon
    ¼ cup melted butter
Filling
    1 pound dry cottage cheese
    3 eggs
    1 tablespoon cornstarch
    1 cup sugar
    1⅓ cups plus heavy cream
    1 teaspoon vanilla
    juice of ½ lemon
    cinnamon

Combine graham cracker crumbs, sugar, almonds, cinnamon and butter. Press into an 8x8-inch square pan that has been greased lightly. Chill until ready to use.

Beat cottage cheese and eggs. Blend cornstarch into the sugar and add to the cottage cheese and eggs; beat well. Add the cream and mix thoroughly. Add vanilla and lemon juice; mix. Pour into crust, sprinkle top with cinnamon, and bake at 350° until set but not dry, 30-45 minutes.

9-12 servings

H

Heinerbeiner Omelet

4 tablespoons butter, divided
¼ cup sliced onion
¼ cup sliced zucchini (¼ inch pieces)
¼ cup sliced mushrooms
¼ cup diced green peppers
3 eggs
3 tablespoons water
salt and pepper to taste
¼ cup grated cheddar cheese

Melt 2 tablespoons butter in saucepan and sauté onions, zucchini, mushrooms and green pepper until soft but not brown. Keep warm. Beat eggs, water, salt and pepper. Melt remaining 2 tablespoons butter in a 7- or 9-inch non-stick frying pan; add eggs. While cooking, lift the edges of omelet while tipping the pan, allowing the uncooked eggs to run underneath. When eggs are set, add the sautéed vegetables and cheese. Fold half the omelet over, then slip onto a plate. Serve with sausage or bacon. Can also be topped with cheese or tomato sauce.

1-2 servings

Blue Cheese Ball

1 8-ounce package cream cheese, room
   temperature
½ cup (1 stick) butter, softened
½ cup crumbled blue cheese
2 tablespoons warm milk
½ cup chopped walnuts or pecans

Mix cream cheese, butter, cheese and milk until well blended and smooth. Place the nutmeats on a sheet of plastic wrap or wax paper. Place the cheese mixture on the wrap and form into a ball being careful to cover the outside of the ball with nutmeats. Refrigerate until ready to use. Serve with your favorite crackers.

1 12-ounce ball

Nan's Après-Ski

1 pound ground beef
2 teaspoons butter
¼ cup chopped green onions
1 4-ounce can green chilis, chopped
1 teaspoon Worcestershire sauce
16 ounces Velveeta Cheese, cubed
dash garlic powder

Sauté beef in butter until browned. Drain. In a double boiler combine the ground beef, onions, chilis, Worcestershire sauce, Velveeta and garlic powder. Heat until cheese melts. Keep warm in chafing dish. Serve with potato chips, tortilla chips or bagel chips.

3 cups

Cucumber Rounds

bread
butter
cream cheese
dry Italian salad dressing mix
cucumber
mayonnaise
radishes
parsley

Cut 2-inch rounds of bread. Make a mixture of 1 part butter with 1 part cream cheese. Add enough dry Italian salad mix to make a tasty blend. Spread mixture on bread rounds, add a slice of peeled cucumber, and top with a dab of mayonnaise. On one half of top add shredded radishes, on the other half put minced parsley. Makes a very colorful hors d'oeuvre.

Easy, Easy Buffalo Wings

24 chicken wings, with wing tips
   removed
1 cup chicken broth
1-1½ cups barbecue sauce
2 tablespoons brown sugar

Arrange chicken wings on a cookie sheet with sides. Add chicken broth just to cover bottom of pan. Bake uncovered at 350º for 20 - 25 minutes or until tender. Arrange the cooked wings on a cookie sheet with 1-inch sides. Combine barbecue sauce and brown sugar. Pour over chicken wings. Broil until browned.

24 appetizers

Chicken Liver Pâté

1 pound chicken livers, washed well
⅔ cup chopped onion
1 clove garlic, crushed
2 bay leaves
1½ cups water
½ teaspoon salt
1½ pounds butter, cut in small pieces
2 teaspoons cognac (optional)

Bring the chicken livers, onion, garlic, bay leaves, water and salt to a boil. Continue to cook for 20-25 minutes or until tender.

Strain liquid and remove bay leaves. Cool thoroughly. In a processor with a steel blade or blender, blend the boiled ingredients while adding butter and cognac. Process until very smooth. Will freeze well but must be brought to room temperature before serving. Excellent served with Lavosh Crackers, recipe on page 57.

2½ cups

Beef Bouillon Dip

1 teaspoon beef bouillon
1 tablespoon hot water
1 8-ounce package cream cheese, softened
1 teaspoon finely grated onion
cream

Dissolve bouillon in hot water. Stir in cream cheese and onion. Blend in enough cream to make mixture a dipping consistency.

1 cup

Barbecued Chinese Chicken Wings

2 cloves garlic, minced
1 tablespoon sugar
½ teaspoon powdered ginger
6 tablespoons soy sauce
3 tablespoons cider vinegar
6 tablespoons honey
2 tablespoons white wine
1 ½ cups beef broth
3 pounds chicken wings

Mix garlic, sugar, ginger, soy sauce, vinegar, honey wine and broth together. Add the wings and marinate 3 hours or overnight. Drain wings, reserving the marinade. Arrange in shallow pan. Bake uncovered at 350° for 20 minutes. Add marinade and bake, basting often, until nicely browned and cooked through.

3 dozen

For Brie Lovers

Remove crust from bread slices and cut into triangle shapes. Cut brie into similar sized wedges. Toast bread on one side. Place wedge of brie on untoasted side, then cover with slivered almonds. Broil until cheese starts to melt. Yummy!!

Herbed Bread Mitzie

1 loaf unsliced bread
1 cup (2 sticks) butter, softened
½ teaspoon paprika
¼ teaspoon rosemary
¼ teaspoon oregano
¼ teaspoon basil
¼ teaspoon garlic salt

Remove crust from all but bottom of bread loaf. Being careful not to cut through the bottom, cut lengthwise down center of the loaf. Then turn and cut crosswise in 1-inch slices.

Mix the butter, paprika, rosemary, oregano, basil and garlic salt together. Spread between the slices of bread and across the top. Bake until golden brown in an uncovered roasting pan at 325° for approximately 2 hours. Remove from pan and complete slicing.

20 pieces

Note…
Can be prepared early in the day, put back in pan and reheated before serving.

Hickory Nut Cake

1 cup shortening or butter, or ½ cup each
2 cups sugar
3 cups cake flour
4 teaspoons baking powder
1 teaspoon salt
1⅓ cups skim milk
2 teaspoons vanilla
6 egg whites (¾ cup)
1 cup hickory nuts

Cream shortening; add sugar and blend well. Sift the flour, baking powder and salt in a separate bowl. Add alternately with milk to creamed mixture. Beat egg whites until stiff. Fold into batter.

Spray and line with wax paper three 8-inch cake pans or two 9-inch cake pans. Turn batter into pans. Bake at 350° for 30-35 minutes or until a toothpick inserted comes out clean.

Spread Butter Cream Frosting (page 116) between layers and on sides and top of cake. Sprinkle with chopped hickory nuts.

12 servings

Note…
This recipe works equally well with pecans, walnuts, pistachios or any other favorite nuts.

As a young person one of my favorite times of the year was fall when nut-picking time arrived. I would help gather the nuts for drying and finally we'd crack a pan full on a long winter's night. I must admit, I ate more than I left for Mom for baking!

I is for Aunt Isabelle with whom Nell lived ("A hundred years ago!") while working for a photographer in Milwaukee. Like Nell's mother, Isabelle's older sister, "Isay," was and still is a great cook and great lady. Especially memorable were Isabelle's Tuesday evening meals where family members including "The Tuesday Night Shadow" gathered to "feast and gab." Nell is grateful to her aunt for the use of her recipes in this section of the book.

R·e·c·i·p·e·s

Isabelle's:

Baking Powder Biscuits

2 cups flour
3 teaspoons baking powder
½ teaspoon salt
4 tablespoons shortening
¾ cup milk

Combine flour, baking powder and salt. Cut in the shortening. Add milk and knead lightly. Roll out ½ inch thick. Cut with 2-inch cookie cutter. Reshape scraps and cut. Arrange on ungreased cookie sheet and bake at 450º for 12-15 minutes or until golden brown. Pass the honey or strawberry butter!

1 dozen

Pepper Relish

    1 dozen red bell peppers
    1 dozen green bell peppers
    14 large onions
    1 cup vinegar
    boiling water
Brine
    1 quart vinegar
    2 cups water
    4 cups sugar
    3 tablespoons salt
    2 tablespoons mustard seed
    2 tablespoons celery seed
    1 teaspoon alum

In a food processor, grind together the peppers and onions. Pour boiling water over peppers and onions to cover; let stand 10 minutes. Drain.

Bring vinegar and 2 cups water to a boil. Add pepper and onion mixture. Boil 3 minutes, then drain.

Brine
Bring brine ingredients to a boil, add peppers and boil 10 minutes. Put in jars and seal. Process in hot water bath for 10 minutes.

    8 pints

Note...
To protect hands, wear rubber gloves while preparing the peppers.

Creamed Eggs on Toast
My favorite when visiting Aunt Isabelle

    3 tablespoons butter
    3 tablespoons flour
    1 teaspoon onion juice or finely-grated
        onion (optional)
    2½ cups milk
    salt and pepper to taste
    5 hard-boiled eggs
    8 slices toast

Melt butter in saucepan; add flour and cook for 2 minutes without browning. Add onion juice and milk. Cook until slightly thickened. Add salt and pepper.

Slice eggs in half. Remove yolks and reserve. Chop egg whites and add to white sauce.

Cut two pieces of toast into triangles, arranging them creatively on a plate. Top with white sauce. Press the reserved yolks through a fine sieve. Sprinkle over sauce. Garnish with a sprinkle of parsley or finely-sliced green onion tops. Happy eating!

4 servings

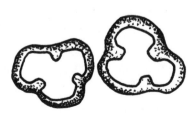

Never-Fail Dumplings

1 egg
milk
2 cups flour
2 teaspoons baking powder
1 teaspoon salt
2 tablespoons butter

Beat egg in measuring cup and add milk to make 1 full cup liquid. Combine dry ingredients and cut in butter. Add milk mixture. Stir just until mixed. Drop by spoonfuls on top of simmering stew or pork hocks and sauerkraut in a saucepan. Cover and continue to simmer for 15 minutes.

6-8 dumplings

Sauerbraten

2 teaspoons salt
1 teaspoon powdered ginger
2 cups cider vinegar
2½ cups water
8 whole cloves
2 medium onions, sliced
2 tablespoons mixed pickling spice
2 bay leaves
1 teaspoon peppercorns
⅓ cup sugar
4 pounds round-bone chuck roast or
   venison
2 tablespoons oil
1 dozen gingersnaps, crumbled

Combine salt, ginger, vinegar, water, cloves, onions, pickling spice, bay leaves, peppercorns and sugar and bring to a boil. Pour over meat and marinate in refrigerator for 3 or 4 days, turning each day. Strain liquid and save.

In roasting pan add oil and brown meat. Add liquid and simmer until meat is tender, 1-1½ hours. (This can be done on top of the stove or in a 350° oven.) Remove the meat. Thicken liquid with gingersnaps. Serve with spaeztles. (Recipe on page 73.)

8 servings

Note...
If you have a venison roast in your freezer and you're not sure how to prepare it, try this recipe. It can fool even a connoisseur!

Beef Birds

2 pounds round steak, about ½ inch
   thick (approximately 8 pieces)
4 slices bacon, cut in small pieces
4 tablespoons finely chopped onion
salt and pepper
flour
2 tablespoons butter
1 teaspoon oil

Trim fat from steak and cut in pieces about 2 inches by 4 inches. Pound thin.

Mix bacon and onion and divide between pieces of meat. Fold meat around filling and secure with tooth-picks or string.

Salt and pepper birds and roll in flour, covering all sides completely. Shake off any excess. Heat butter and oil in a roasting pan; brown birds on all sides. Add water to, but not quite covering, birds. Cover pan and simmer for 1 hour or until tender. Check seasonings of gravy. Serve with dumplings or spaetzles.

4-6 servings

The Tuesday Night Shadow's Favorite!

Peanut Squares

½ cup butter
1 cup sugar
1 ½ cups flour
2 teaspoons baking powder
½ cup milk
1 teaspoon vanilla
4 egg whites

Butter Cream Frosting
1½ cups butter, softened
4 cups confectioners' sugar, sifted
2 tablespoons milk
1 teaspoon vanilla
1 pound unsalted peanuts, shelled and chopped

Cream butter and sugar until light. Mix flour and baking powder together. Add to the butter, mixing in alternately with milk. Add vanilla and mix well.

Beat egg whites until stiff but not dry. Fold into batter. Bake in a well-buttered 9x13-inch pan at 325° for 25-30 minutes or until done. Cool.

Beat butter, confectioners' sugar, milk and vanilla on low until well blended then beat on high until fluffy, a total of 4-5 minutes.

Cut cake in squares; frost top and sides of each square, then roll in peanuts.

24 squares

Schaum Torte

9 egg whites
3 cups sugar
1½ teaspoons cream of tartar
1½ teaspoons vinegar
1 teaspoon vanilla

Preheat oven to 500°. Mix together all ingredients. Beat with a mixer for 25 minutes. Put in greased 10-inch springform pan. Place in oven and turn off heat. Leave all night, approximately 8-10 hours. No peeking!

Serve covered with fresh sweetened strawberries or peaches and top with whipped cream. Garnish with fruit slices and a sprig of mint.

10 servings

Nell's White Cake with Aunt Isabelle's Treatment

Aunt Isay took my recipe for white cake and added poppy seeds. She soaks the seeds in half of the milk for 10 minutes while she begins creaming the shortening...

Cake
- ¾ cup poppy seed (for Isay's Treatment)
- 1½ cups milk (divided for Isay's Treatment)
- ¾ cup shortening (butter, margarine or Crisco)
- 2 cups white sugar, divided
- 3¼ cups flour
- 4 ½ teaspoons baking powder
- ½ teaspoon salt
- 2 teaspoons vanilla
- 4 large egg whites (½ cup)

Lemon Filling
- 1½ tablespoons cornstarch
- ½ cup sugar
- dash salt
- 1 cup milk
- 2 egg yolks, beaten
- scant ¼ cup lemon juice
- ½ teaspoon grated lemon rind
- 1½ tablespoons butter

Frosting
- 3 heaping tablespoons flour
- 1 cup milk
- 1 cup sugar
- 1 cup butter
- 1 teaspoon vanilla

If preparing poppy seed cake, soak poppy seeds in ¾ cup milk for 10 minutes. To make cake, cream the shortening, gradually adding 1½ cups of the sugar. Beat until fluffy. Sift flour, baking powder and salt. Add sifted ingredients to shortening and sugar alternately with the milk or milk and poppy seed mixtue. Add vanilla.

Beat egg whites until frothy. Gradually add the remaining ½ cup sugar, beating until stiff. Fold into the above mixture. Divide into two greased and floured 9-inch cake pans. Bake at 350° for 25-30 minutes or until tester comes out clean.

For filling, mix cornstarch, sugar and salt. Add milk. Cook over low heat until thick, remove from heat and add beaten egg yolks. Return to heat and cook for 2 minutes. Remove and add lemon juice, rind and butter, stirring well. Cool completely. Spread between layers of cake.

For frosting, mix flour and milk together in a saucepan. Cook over medium heat until thick, then cool. Cream sugar, butter and vanilla together, add flour mixture, and beat until fluffy. Frost cake. 12-14 servings

J

Jambogumby

¼ cup butter
1 cup chopped onion
1 cup chopped green or red pepper or combination
2 cloves garlic
½ teaspoon thyme
½ teaspoon oregano
1 bay leaf
1 28-ounce can stewed tomatoes
⅛ teaspoon cayenne
½ teaspoon chili power
1 15-ounce can tomato sauce
1 pound hot sausage (Italian or Andouille)
1½ pounds raw shrimp

Melt butter in saucepan and sauté onion and pepper until tender. Add garlic, thyme, oregano, bay leaf, tomatoes, cayenne, chili powder and tomato sauce. Simmer covered for 15 minutes. Meanwhile sauté sausage until lightly browned and prick to extract the fat from the sausage. Cut into one-inch pieces and add to the pot. Continue to cook for another 15 minutes. Add cleaned raw shrimp and continue cooking for about 5 minutes. Remove bay leaf. Serve over cooked rice. Garnish with fresh-cut onion tops or chives.

6 servings

Jalapeno and Cheese Buns

4-4¾ cups flour
½ pound grated cheddar cheese
½ cup finely chopped jalapeno peppers
1¼-ounce package dry yeast
1½ cups milk (105-115º), divided
½ cup sugar
½ cup vegetable oil
1 egg, slightly beaten
1 teaspoon salt

Combine 4 cups of flour, cheese and peppers. Dissolve yeast in ½ cup warm milk; let stand 5 minutes. In a large bowl add remaining milk, sugar, oil and egg. Gradually add the flour mixture to the yeast mixture, using a bread hook if you have one. Add enough of the reserved ¾ cup of flour to make a soft, but not sticky, dough.

Turn dough out onto lightly floured surface and knead about 10 minutes. Put dough into greased bowl, cover and let rise until doubled, about 45 minutes. Punch down. Form dough into 12 balls; place into greased cake tins so that they are just touching. Cover and let rise until doubled. Bake at 350º for 25-30 minutes or until nicely browned.

1 dozen

Johnny Cake

1 cup cornmeal
1½ tablespoons sugar
¾ teaspoon salt
1 cup boiling water
½ cup sifted flour
2 teaspoons baking powder
1 egg
½ cup milk
2 tablespoons butter, melted

In a large bowl, combine cornmeal, sugar and salt. Slowly add boiling water. Cover and let stand about 10 minutes. Sift together flour and baking powder. In a small bowl, beat egg with milk and butter until well blended. Pour into cornmeal mixture. Add flour mixture; stir quickly just to combine.

Cook on a lightly greased, heated griddle or skillet, using about ¼ cup batter for each cake; cook until bubbles form and edges become dry. Flip; cook about 1½-2 minutes longer or until nicely browned.

10 pancakes

Note…
Serve with maple syrup, whipped butter, applesauce, fresh fruit, sour cream with brown sugar, or your favorite jam.

To create a nice brown roll, beat together one egg and one teaspoon of water. Brush over rolls before baking.

Judy's Potato Casserole

  5 pounds potatoes, peeled and cubed
  1 8-ounce package cream cheese
  1 cup half-and-half
  2 tablespoons grated onion
  ½ cup margarine
  1 teaspoon savory salt (1 teaspoon salt
     and ¼ teaspoon pepper mixed to-
     gether)
  1 teaspoon seasoned salt (Lawry's)
  2 tablespoons butter, melted
  paprika

Cook potatoes in water to cover until very soft. Drain. Beat cheese and half-and-half with mixer. Add potatoes, onion, margarine, salt and pepper, and seasoned salt; mash well. Put in buttered, 2½-quart casserole. Brush top with butter, sprinkle with paprika and bake at 350º for 30 minutes.

12 servings

Jelly Roll and Some Inspirations

4 eggs, separated
¾ cup sugar, divided
1 tablespoon vegetable oil
⅔ cup sifted cake flour
scant ½ teaspoon salt
1 teaspoon baking powder
powdered sugar

Grease a 15x10-inch jelly roll pan and line with parchment or wax paper. Grease and flour paper. Set aside.

Beat egg whites until frothy then gradually add ½ cup of sugar. Set aside. With the same beaters, beat the yolks and remaining ¼ cup sugar until light and fluffy. Add the vegetable oil. Fold in egg whites.

Combine flour, salt and baking powder. Gradually fold into egg mixture. Pour into prepared pan and bake at 350° for 10-12 minutes or until very light brown.

Sprinkle powdered sugar on clean towel or parchment paper and unmold baked jelly roll. Carefully peel off paper. Start rolling from narrow end and roll cake and towel together. With seam-side down, cover and let cake cool completely. Unroll cake, remove from towel and fill with one of the following inspirations.

8-10 servings

Inspiration #1

2 cups sliced strawberries and 2 cups whipped cream. Reroll and top with a sprinkle of powdered sugar and decorate with strawberries. Refrigerate until serving time.

Inspiration #2

Fill with ice cream. Return to freezer and freeze until solid. Serve cut in slices topped with chocolate sauce, raspberry sauce, caramel or butterscotch.

Inspiration #3

Substitute lemon flavoring for vanilla in jelly roll, then prepare the following:

Lemon Filling
    1 cup sugar
    ½ cup cornstarch
    dash salt
    1½ cups water
    3 egg yolks, beaten
    1 teaspoon grated lemon rind
    ⅓ cup lemon juice
    1 tablespoon butter

Combine sugar, cornstarch and dash of salt; add water and heat to boiling, stirring constantly, until thickened. Remove from heat and slowly add the beaten egg yolks; return to heat and stir constantly for 2 minutes. Add lemon rind, lemon juice and butter; stir to blend. Cool completely. Spread in roll. Roll up. At this point the roll can be refrigerated, covered, for several hours or overnight. When ready to serve, sprinkle with powdered sugar and garnish with very thin slices of lemon.

Inspiration #4

Chocolate Bûche de Nöel
Follow the original recipe but add 3 tablespoons cocoa sifted with flour. Proceed as recipe describes but when rolling, roll from the long end instead of short end.

Filling and Frosting
Chocolate Butter Cream
Use the butter cream frosting under X-Rated Torte on page 116. Melt 3 ounces unsweetened chocolate and add to the egg mixture before adding butter.

Frost inside of jelly roll and carefully roll up. Cut approximately 2 inches off each end of roll at angle and attach to side of cake roll log to form branches. Frost with remainder of filling. With fork make lines to resemble bark. Garnish with meringue mushrooms.

Meringue Mushrooms
    2 egg whites
    ½ cup sugar

Preheat oven to 250º. Line baking sheet with parchment. Beat egg whites until stiff peaks form. Add sugar slowly, beating very well. Spoon into pastry bag fitted with plain tip. Pipe small peaked rounds for stems. Make some slightly larger and smooth tops with moist clean finger. Bake 1½ hours or until dry and very slightly browned. Cool on rack. With a pointed knife make a small hole in bottom of larger round, spread a small amount of chocolate filling and add stem, then place on rack to set. Dust top very lightly with cocoa.

Bûche de Nöel

Jerry's Creamy Frosting

¾ cup shortening, not butter
¼ teaspoon salt
⅓ cup non-fat dry milk
½ cup water
1 teaspoon vanilla
1¾ pounds confectioners' sugar (7 cups more or less)

Combine all ingredients and mix at medium speed for 3 minutes. Increase speed to high and beat 5 minutes more.

Excellent frosting for decorating. Leftover frosting can be stored in a tightly-covered bowl and refrigerated. Keeps for weeks. To use, set out until it reaches room temperature.

2 cups

Jimminy Cricket's Divinity

3 cups sugar
½ cup light corn syrup
¾ cup water
½ teaspoon salt
1 teaspoon vanilla
2 egg whites, room temperature
1 cup chopped nuts, reserving large pieces for garnish

Combine sugar, corn syrup and water in saucepan. Cook over low heat, stirring until sugar is dissolved. Increase heat; bring to boiling. Cover and boil, without stirring, 3 minutes. (This avoids wiping crystals from pan.) Uncover and continue cooking until a candy thermometer reaches 258°. (Or when a small amount dropped into cold water forms a very firm ball.) Remove from heat.

Add salt and vanilla to egg whites. Beat on high speed until stiff moist peaks form. Slowly beat in hot syrup in a thin stream holding pan several inches above whites. Continue beating until mixture holds its shape but is still glossy. Add nuts. Drop by teaspoons on wax paper or spread in a pan and cut into squares. Garnish with nuts.

Store in a tightly covered container.

2 dozen

By the Author

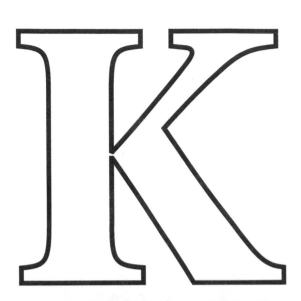

K

R·e·c·i·p·e·s

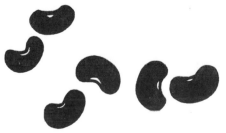

Ken's Pea Soup

 2 pounds split peas
 1 tablespoon salt
 1 ham bone and ½ pound diced ham
 4 cups diced onions
 1 cup diced bell pepper
 2 cups diced celery
 2 cups diced potatoes
 4 quarts water
 pepper to taste

Simmer peas, salt, ham bone and diced ham, onions, pepper and celery in water for 2 hours. Add potatoes and simmer for another 1 hour, adding more water if needed.

Remove ham bone. Adjust seasonings.

10-12 servings

Kidney Bean Salad

4 hard-boiled eggs
1 16-ounce can light or dark kidney
   beans
⅓ cup pickle relish
¼ cup finely chopped onion
mayonnaise
stuffed olives (optional)

Chop 3 of the hard-boiled eggs. Drain beans, add chopped eggs, pickle relish, chopped onion and enough mayonnaise to moisten. Mix. Garnish top with slices of reserved egg and slices of stuffed olives if desired.

4 servings

Kate's Potatoes
a la Swiss Cheese

8 medium potatoes, sliced thin
salt and pepper
¼ cup finely chopped onion
1½ cups grated Swiss cheese
6 tablespoons butter
1¼ cups chicken stock

Butter a 9x12-inch glass dish. Arrange half of the potatoes in dish, sprinkle with salt and pepper. Add the onions and half the cheese. Dot with half of the butter. Add the rest of the potatoes, butter and cheese. Pour chicken stock over top.

Bake at 375º for 30 minutes or until potatoes are tender and have a golden crust.

6-8 servings

Note...
To keep potatoes from darkening, put the slices in cold water but be sure to drain them well before putting in the glass dish.

Karta's Potato Salad

5 pounds new red potatoes
1½ cups chopped celery
2 tablespoons grated onion
3 tablespoons white wine vinegar
2 tablespoons sugar
1 tablespoon yellow mustard
1 tablespoon Dijon mustard
1 teaspoon salt
2 cups mayonnaise
1 cup sour cream
6 hard-boiled eggs, reserve 1 for garnish

Scrub potatoes, then boil until tender. Leaving skins on, cut into cubes; add chopped celery. Combine the onion, vinegar, sugar, mustards, salt, mayonnaise and sour cream and mix well. Add to potatoes, stirring gently to mix. Chop eggs and add; mix again.

Garnish with slices of the reserved egg.

12-14 servings

Kirsch and Cherry
Pork Chops

4 center cut pork chops, ½ inch thick
2 tablespoons oil
1 16-ounce can dark, sweet, pitted
   cherries
½ tablespoon cornstarch mixed with
   small amount of water
3 tablespoons Kirsch liqueur

Slowly sauté chops in oil until they are tender. Drain cherries, reserving liquid. Heat cherry liquid in saucepan and thicken slightly with cornstarch and water. When thickened add cherries and Kirsch liquor. Pour over the chops and reheat. Serve.

4 servings

Keen Ways with Crêpes
Basic Crepe Batter

1½ cups flour
1 teaspoon sugar
⅛ teaspoon salt
3 eggs
1½ cups milk
2 tablespoons butter, melted

Combine flour, sugar and salt. Beat eggs well. Add dry ingredients alternately with milk to eggs, beating until smooth. Add butter and beat to mix. If mixture seems too thick, add a little more liquid. The consistency should be no thicker than heavy cream.

Use a 5- to 7-inch sauté pan (non-stick coating preferred) with sloping sides. Preheat pan and brush very lightly with oil. Remove pan from heat. Using a spoon or ladle that holds just enough batter (2 tablespoons for 6-inch pan) add batter and quickly tilt pan so batter flows to coat bottom of the pan. If you pour too much in, just pour off excess. Return pan to heat and cook for about 1 minute. Check to see if lightly browned. Flip over and cook for about ½ minute. If crêpes are to be used immediately, stack and keep warm in oven. If to be used later, stack crêpes between sheets of wax paper. Crêpes may also be frozen for later use.

Yield: 25-30 5-inch crêpes
        15-20 6-inch crêpes

Note…
Additional flavorings can be added to the batter such as:
  1 tablespoon dill weed
  1 tablespoon Italian seasonings
  1 tablespoon basil, oregano, or parsley
  flakes

Basic White Sauce

4 tablespoons butter
2 tablespoons minced onion
2 tablespoons minced red or green
  pepper
4 tablespoons flour
3 cups milk, chicken broth or
  half of each
salt and pepper

Melt butter; add onions and pepper. Sauté until soft. Add flour and cook over medium heat for 1-2 minutes. Add the milk or broth and simmer until thickened. Add salt and pepper.

Crab, Shrimp or Lobster Filled Crêpes

2 cups cooked crab, shrimp or lobster
  (or a combination)
Basic White Sauce
12 crepes
½ cup Parmesan cheese

Stir the seafood into half of the basic white sauce. Spoon 1-2 tablespoons of this mixture down the center of each crêpe. Roll and place seam side down in a large baking dish. Top with remaining sauce. Sprinkle with cheese. Bake at 375° for 15-20 minutes or until bubbly and lightly browned.

6 servings

Note…
Other additions to Basic White Sauce could be:

> 1 pound mushrooms, sliced and sautéed
> 1 pound cooked asparagus or broccoli
> 1½ cups chopped ham
> 1½ cups chopped chicken or turkey

Or a portion of two or three of the above. An example: leftover chicken and broccoli combined give a different taste.

Crêpes are a great way to use leftovers and the imagination!

Dessert Crêpes

> 12 crepes
> sliced strawberries, peaches, pineapple, or bananas

Fill crêpes with 1½-2 tablespoons of fresh fruit. Roll. Place on dessert plates. Top with sweetened whipped cream or scoop of vanilla ice cream. Garnish with maraschino cherry halves, chopped nuts, warmed fudge or caramel sauce. Yummy!

6-12 servings

Note…
Flavorings that can be added to the basic crepe recipe for dessert crêpes are:

> 1 teaspoon vanilla extract
> 1 teaspoon almond extract
> 1 teaspoon brandy or other liqueurs

Ken's Ground Beef Rolls

> 1 pound ground beef
> 1 egg
> 1½ teaspoons salt, divided
> ½ teaspoon pepper, plus additional to taste
> 4 slices bread, softened in small amount of water
> 2 tablespoons minced onion
> 1 cup fresh mushrooms, cut or
>   1 7-ounce can, drained
> ½ teaspoon thyme
> 1 10¾-ounce can mushroom soup

Combine meat, egg, 1 teaspoon of salt and ½ teaspooon pepper. Divide meat into 6 portions. Place each portion on a piece of waxed paper, cover with another sheet of paper and press into a 5x5-inch square.

Combine bread, onions, mushrooms, thyme and remaining salt and pepper. Mix well. Spoon mixture onto squares of meat from one corner to the opposite corner. Then fold the two remaining corners over the filling. Place in a lightly greased 9x13-inch baking dish.

Heat the mushroom soup with half a can of water. Mix well. Pour over meat. Bake at 350° for approximately 45 minutes, or until bubbly and lightly browned.

6 small servings

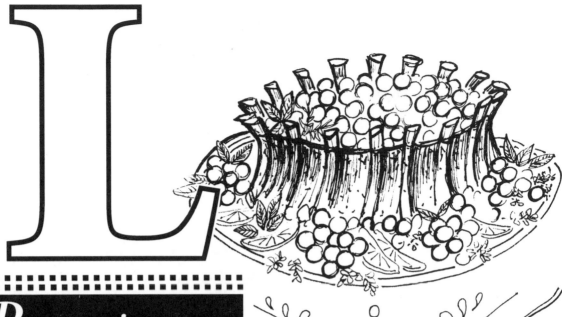

L

Lamb Rack

¼ cup Dijon mustard
1½ teaspoons soy sauce
1 clove garlic, minced
¼ teaspoon dried marjoram
⅛ teaspoon powdered ginger
1 lamb rack (4-6 ribs)

Mix mustard, soy sauce, garlic, marjoram and ginger together. Place meat in roasting pan and roast at 375º for 25-30 minutes or until done. If drippings start to brown during baking, add small amount of water.

2 servings

Liver Dumpling Soup

1 pound beef liver
3 sprigs parsley
1 medium onion
2 tablespoons oil
⅓ - ½ cup bread crumbs
2 or 3 tablespoons flour
1 egg, beaten
salt and pepper
1 teaspoon basil
8 cups well-seasoned chicken broth, your
  own or canned

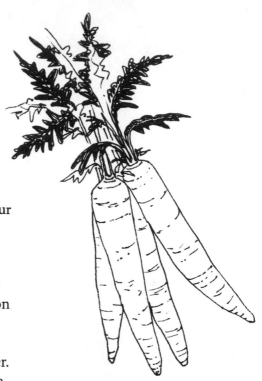

Sear the liver to facilitate grinding. Grind or process with a steel blade liver and parsley sprigs. Sauté the onion in oil until tender, not browned. Add onions, ⅓ cup crumbs, 2 tablespoons flour, egg, salt, pepper and basil to liver. (The less stiffening used, the better the dumpling.) Form mixture into egg-sized dumplings.

Test one dumpling in boiling, salted water. If it keeps its shape, cook the others. Add more of the crumbs and flour if dumplings do not hold their shape when boiled. Boil gently 5-6 minutes.

Add one or two dumplings to a well-seasoned chicken broth.

8-10 servings

Note...
These dumplings also make a nice addition to pork hocks and sauerkraut or pork chops.

Lemon Carrots

1 pound carrots
¾ cup chicken broth
2 tablespoons sugar
2 tablespoons butter
grated rind of 1 lemon
2 tablespoons lemon juice
chopped parsley (optional)

Cut carrots lengthwise in strips about 2½ inches long. Place carrot strips in small saucepan and stir in chicken broth, sugar, butter, lemon rind and lemon juice. Bring mixture to boil, cover and simmer 20 minutes. Place in serving bowl and garnish with chopped parsley if desired.

6-8 servings

Lamb Shanks

4 lamb shanks
salt and pepper
¼ cup Worcestershire sauce
2 carrots
2 ribs celery
1 medium onion
2 cups water
2 cups white wine
1½ tablespoons cornstarch dissolved in
    small amount of water

Season lamb shanks with salt and pepper and place in roasting pan. Brush with Worcestershire sauce. Bake at 350º until nicely browned, about 1 hour.

Process carrots, celery and onion with steel blade, or grind until fine. Add to the browned shanks along with water and wine. Cover and bake an additional 1 hour or until tender. Strain juices and degrease. Thicken liquid with cornstarch. Adjust seasoning. Serve over shanks.

4 servings

Lavosch Crackers

2 cups water
2¼-ounce packages dry yeast
3 tablespoons honey
½ cup butter or margarine, melted
3½-4 cups white flour
1½ teaspoons salt
2 cups whole wheat flour

Heat water to 110-115º. Add dry yeast and honey. Set aside for 5 minutes. In a large bowl or in mixer bowl with dough hook, combine melted butter, 2 cups white flour, salt and yeast mixture. Stir or mix vigorously until the dough is smooth and soft. Add wheat flour and continue to knead or mix. Add the remaining 1½ cups of white flour. Continue to knead until you have a smooth and soft dough.

Place dough in an oiled bowl and let rise until doubled in bulk. Punch down and separate into 8 pieces. Roll and stretch each piece until dough is almost paper thin. Place on ungreased cookie sheet. With a fork make many little holes over the surface. Bake at 350º for 5-7 minutes, turn and bake another 5-7 minutes until lightly browned. When cold, break into pieces.

40 pieces, approximately

My favorite way to prepare lamb chops is to lightly broil them until nicely browned. I love the flavor of lamb so it needs no additions!

Let's Talk Sandwiches

The sandwich is part of everyday life. There are so many variations that can make the ordinary sandwich more attractive and tasty. Presentation is equally important. Eat with your eyes! Add a garnish. Use whatever is available: attractively arranged pickle slices with a radish rose, carrot and celery sticks, green onions, or any fruit with mint or parsley sprigs. Bunches of grapes or parsley alone can do wonders! The following will give you some ideas how to make a sandwich fit for a king – let's not leave out the queen!

Start with good breads: pocket bread, seven-grain bread, herbed bread, dill, sourdough, pumpernickel, gourmet rye, or raisin for chicken salad. Don't forget buns: onion, cheese, wheat, sourdough, focaccia, tortillas, crescent, or plain white if you prefer.

Cold Sandwiches
Fillings: lettuce, tomatoes, sprouts, spinach, sliced onion or cheeses: brie, blue, cheddar, Swiss or any other favorite.
Toppings: 1 tablespoon of ranch, poppy seed, garlic or Italian dressing.

Hot Meat Sandwiches
Seasonings: Cajun, Italian, minced herbs, garlic powder, onion powder, Worcestershire, Tabasco.
Toppings: cooked bacon, chopped peppers, salsa, chopped stuffed olives, sliced tomato, chopped lettuce, hot peppers, mozzarella, dill, havarti, Swiss or any other cheese, sautéed mushrooms, sauerkraut. Combine your favorites!

Chicken or Turkey, Shrimp, Crab or Tuna Salad
Additions to the dressing: dill, seasoning salt, capers, small amount of mustard or tarragon.
Toppings: tomato, lettuce, sprouts, chopped pecans, walnuts, sunflower seeds, pine nuts.

Sautéed Chicken Breast

Sauté a seasoned chicken breast. Toast a slice of your favorite bread, cut into toast points and arrange on a plate. Top with as many of the following as desired: lettuce, tomato, bacon, ham, shrimp. Add the sautéed chicken cut in strips; top off with 1 tablespoon salsa, blue cheese, garlic dressing, French dressing, or your favorite. Then sprinkle with sautéed almonds, cashews, cut green onion tops, chives or red onion slices. Serve open-faced. Be creative, and don't forget the garnish!

Libby's Lemon Bread

  6 tablespoons butter
  1½ cups sugar, divided
  1½ cups flour
  1 teaspoon baking powder
  ¼ teaspoon salt
  2 eggs
  ½ cup milk
  1 cup chopped nuts
  grated rind of 2 lemons
  ¼ cup lemon juice

Cream butter and 1 cup sugar. Sift together flour, baking powder and salt. Add to creamed mixture with eggs, milk, nuts and grated peel. Mix very lightly until flour is absorbed. Spoon batter into a greased 5x9-inch bread tin. Bake at 350° for 65 minutes. As soon as it is done, mix remaining ½ cup sugar and lemon juice.

Poke holes in the top and pour mixture over bread. Cool before removing from pan.

Yield: 1 loaf

Note...
Libby makes this the day before and wraps it in foil, then refrigerates.

A favorite sandwich of my daughter, Cindy, when she invited a friend for lunch, was open-faced burgers. Mix a small amount of ketchup and mustard with ground beef. Split rolls in half and spread the mixture out thinly, all the way to the edges. Broil until nicely browned. Try it —— kids love them!

Lady Fingers

3 eggs, separated
⅓ cup plus 3 tablespoons sugar, divided
1 teaspoon vanilla
½ teaspoon lemon extract
⅔ cup flour
dash salt
confectioners' sugar

Grease and flour two large cookie sheets or cover with parchment paper. Beat egg yolks with ⅓ cup of sugar and vanilla until very thick and light. Add lemon extract. Sift flour and fold into mixture. Beat egg whites and salt, then gradually add remaining sugar. Beat until stiff and glossy. Stir ¼ of the whites into the egg mixture. Then fold in remaining whites. Spoon batter into pastry bag with a large plain tip. Press into strips ½ inch wide by 3 inches long. Sprinkle with confectioners' sugar. Bake at 325° 15-20 minutes or until delicate, golden brown. Transfer to wire rack and sprinkle again with confectioners' sugar.

2 dozen

There are times when a recipe refuses to perform. This once happened when the lady fingers spread out more than I wanted. They could have been saved by trimming, but two young guests laughed at the odd shapes and ate them as fast as they came out of the oven. Their fun was worth a trip to the market to buy packaged lady fingers!

Lady Finger Torte

2 dozen purchased split lady fingers, or make your own
¼ cup liqueur, Amaretto, Kahlua or any other favorite
12 ounces semi-sweet chocolate
2 8-ounce packages cream cheese, softened
½ cup sugar
3 eggs, separated
2 teaspoons vanilla
2 cups whipped cream

Line bottom and sides of 10-inch springform pan with split lady fingers. Brush lady fingers with the liqueur.

Melt chocolate in double boiler. Cool.

Beat cream cheese and sugar until light and fluffy. Add egg yolks, beating well. Stir in melted chocolate and vanilla.

Beat egg whites until stiff and fold into chocolate mixture. Fold in whipped cream.

Pour half of mixture into the prepared pan, add a layer of lady fingers. Pour in remainder of filling. Cover and chill overnight. Garnish with whipped cream and sprinkles of grated chocolate.

12 servings

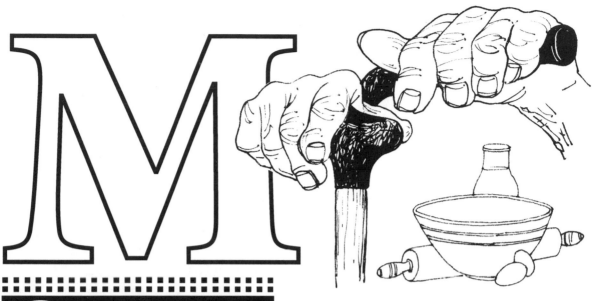

M

R·e·c·i·p·e·s

M is for mom – Nell's mom.

Nell recalls many happy childhood memories of pouring over recipes with "Grandma Canes" as she is affectionatly called by her grandchildren. Not only was Nell's mom a great teacher but a wonderful cook as well. From her kitchen emanated an endless parade of scrumptious desserts and breads. But according to Nell, her beef pot roast was "out of this world."

Event though mother and daughter spent countless hours together in the kitchen, Nell laments being unable to duplicate some of the unique and subtle flavors which she attritubes to a mother's touch.

Ham Balls

1½ pounds lean ham, ground
½ pound fresh pork, ground
2 cups crushed cornflakes
1 cup pineapple juice
2 eggs

Sauce

1½ cups brown sugar
1 teaspoon dry mustard
½ cup water
½ cup vinegar

Combine ham, pork, cornflakes, juice and eggs. Form into balls 1½ inches in size, and place in a 10x13-inch baking dish.

For sauce combine sugar, mustard, water and vinegar. Pour over the balls, cover and bake at 300° for 2 hours.

6-8 servings, about 32 balls

Note...
Some revisions to this recipe are: adding ½ medium onion (grated), using orange juice instead of pineapple juice, using half balsamic vinegar and half white vinegar. Any way you do it, this is a great recipe, and a wonderful pot luck dish.

Frosted Prune-Filled Buns

1¼-ounce package dry yeast
2 tablespoons sugar
¼ cup lukewarm water (110-115°)
1 cup warm milk
1 egg, beaten
1 teaspoon salt
3½ - 4 cups flour
egg wash (1 egg beaten with 1 table-
    spoon water)

Dissolve yeast and sugar in water. Set aside for 5 minutes.

In a large bowl, combine milk, egg, salt and 1½ cups flour. Mix well. Add the yeast mixture. Continue adding flour until dough is soft but not sticky. Knead for about 10 minutes, until smooth and elastic. Place in a greased pan and let rise in a draft-free place until doubled in bulk, 1-1½ hours. Punch down and let rise again. Then punch down and divide into 12 equal pieces. Flatten each piece into a circle. Place 3 or 4 cooked prunes in the center and fold dough around the prunes being sure to seal completely.

Place on a greased cookie sheet and let rise again until doubled, about 45 minutes. Brush with egg wash and bake at 400° for 20-25 minutes or until golden brown. When cool, frost with Powdered Sugar Frosting. (See following recipe.)

12 rolls

Note...
Jams may also be substituted for prunes. These buns are also delicious made without any filling at all!

Powdered Sugar Frosting

2 cups powdered sugar
2 tablespoons milk
½ teaspoon vanilla

Mix ingredients together until smooth.

Mom's Pie Crust

3 cups flour
½ teaspoon salt
1 cup shortening
1 egg
water
3 tablespoons lemon juice

Place flour and salt in large bowl. With pastry blender, cut in the shortening until it forms pea-sized pieces. In a measuring cup beat egg and add water to make just a tad over ½ cup, then add the lemon juice. Add liquid mixture to the flour mixture and stir with a fork to gather together, gently forming into a ball. Proceed like any other pie crust.

3 crusts

Delectable Spice Cake

1 teaspoon soda
2⅔ cups flour, sifted
1 teaspoon cinnamon
½ teaspoon ground cloves
¼ teaspoon salt
¼ teaspoon nutmeg
3 cups brown sugar, divided
¾ cup shortening
2 eggs, beaten
1 teaspoon vanilla
1¼ cups buttermilk
2 egg whites
¼ cup chopped pecans

Sift soda, flour, cinnamon, cloves, salt, and nutmeg. In separate bowl, cream sugar and shortening. Add eggs and vanilla. Add dry ingredients alternately with buttermilk to creamed mixture. Spread in a greased 9x13-inch pan.

Beat egg whites until slightly stiff. Add remaining 1 cup brown sugar and continue beating until well blended. Spread on top of batter and top with pecans. Bake 375° at for 35-40 minutes or until toothpick comes out clean.

20 bars

Chocolate Sunday Pie

1½ cups crushed chocolate wafers
6 tablespoons melted butter
1½ cups evaporated milk
½ teaspoon nutmeg
3 eggs, separated
1 tablespoon boiling water
½ cup sugar
pinch salt
1 tablespoon gelatin dissolved in 3 tablespoons cold water
½ teaspoon nutmeg
½ teaspoon vanilla
1 cup whipped cream
¼ cup grated chocolate, semi-sweet or bitter

Combine wafers and melted butter. Pat mixture into a 9-inch pie plate. Set aside.

Heat milk and nutmeg in double boiler. In a separate bowl, beat egg yolks with boiling water. Mix in sugar and salt. Add to hot milk, whisking to blend. Cook until thick as cream. Take from heat and add gelatin and vanilla. Let set at room temperature. If refrigerated, watch carefully so that it doesn't get too thick!

When beginning to set, beat the egg-whites until stiff. Gently fold into the milk mixture. Place in the crust and chill. Serve topped with whipped cream. Sprinkle with grated chocolate.

6-8 servings

Dark Fruit Cake

½ cup dark raisins
1 cup white raisins
1¼ cups chopped dates
1 cup mixed candied fruit - use
   red and green cherries, and pineapple
½ cup currants
½ cup citron (optional)
½ cup wine or fruit juice
1 tablespoon brandy
grated rind of 1 orange
grated rind of 1 lemon
1 cup butter
2 cups light brown sugar
4 eggs, well beaten
3 tablespoons molasses

½ teaspoon salt
½ teaspoon soda
2 teaspoons cinnamon
1 teaspoon ground cloves
½ teaspoon mace
½ teaspoon nutmeg
¼ teaspoon allspice
3 teaspoons baking power
3 cups flour
4 tablespoons coffee (liquid)
¼ cup orange juice
¼ cup lemon juice
1 tablespoon vanilla
¾ cup slivered almonds
1 cup walnut meats

Combine the raisins, dates, candied fruit, currants, citron, wine or fruit juice, brandy and orange and lemon rind. Let stand overnight at room temperature. (This plumps the fruit.)

Cream butter and sugar. Add eggs and molasses and cream. In a separate bowl sift together salt, soda, cinnamon, cloves, mace, nutmeg, allspice, baking powder and flour. Add 1 cup to creamed mixture. Add coffee, fruit juices and vanilla. Cream. Add remaining flour mixture. Fold in soaked fruit and nuts.

Preheat oven to 275º. Grease the bottom and the sides of two 9x5x3-inch pans and line with brown paper or foil. Grease the lining very well. Divide batter between pans. Place a baking rack in roasting pan, half-fill with water, and place the two cake pans on the rack. The water should be half way up the sides of the cake pans. Bake for about 4 hours or until the cake shrinks slightly from the sides of the pan. Cool on a rack for 1 hour. Remove cake from pans and cool right side up until thoroughly cool. Wrap in several layers of rum or brandy-soaked cheesecloth. Then wrap in foil. Store in an airtight container for 3 weeks to age.

If cheesecloth becomes dry, add more rum or brandy. Can be kept for months and can be frozen. Enjoy!!!

2 loaves

Chop Suey Ooh! La! La! Cake

¾ cup chopped dates
¾ cup sugar
¾ cup water
3 cups sifted flour
1½ teaspoons baking soda
1 teaspoon salt
1½ cups sugar
¾ cup vegetable shortening
3 eggs
1¼ cups buttermilk
¾ cup English walnut pieces

Custard Filling

¼ cup sugar
1 tablespoon cornstarch
¼ teaspoon salt
1 cup milk
2 egg yolks, beaten
1 teaspoon vanilla

Caramel Frosting

½ cup butter
1 cup brown sugar
¼ cup milk
2 cups confectioners' sugar

Combine the dates, sugar and water. Cook for 3-5 minutes. Set aside to cool. Sift together the flour, baking soda and salt. Set aside.

Cream together the sugar and shortening. Add the eggs, one at a time, beating well after each addition. Add the buttermilk alternately with the flour mixture, blending thoroughly by hand or with an electric mixer on low speed. Fold in date mixture and walnuts. Pour into 2 well-greased, lightly-floured 9-inch cake pans. Bake at 350º for 35-40 minutes.

Meanwhile, prepare custard filling. In a small bowl, combine sugar, cornstarch and salt. Scald milk, then add slowly to beaten egg yolks. Stir sugar mixture into milk and egg mixture. Cook in top of double boiler until custard coats spoon. Cool. Add vanilla. Spread between cake layers.

To make caramel frosting, melt butter in saucepan. Add brown sugar. Boil over low heat for 2 minutes, stirring constantly. Add milk. Stir until it comes to a boil. Set aside to cool. Add confectioners' sugar gradually, beating well after each addition and continue beating until the right consistency to spread. Ice top and sides of cake. Decorate with walnut halves.

10-12 servings

Suet or Christmas Pudding

1 cup finely ground or chopped suet
1 cup fine dry bread crumbs
1 cup dark corn syrup
2 eggs, beaten
2 cups flour
½ teaspoon salt
2 teaspoons baking powder
¼ teaspoon soda
½ cup sugar
½ teaspoon nutmeg
½ teaspoon cloves
½ teaspoon allspice
1 teaspoon cinnamon
¾ cup milk
1½ cups seedless raisins
¼ cup chopped walnuts

Combine suet and crumbs. Add syrup and eggs and blend. In separate bowl, sift together flour, salt, baking powder, soda, sugar, nutmeg, cloves, allspice and cinnamon. Add dry ingredients alternately with milk to suet mixture. Add raisins and nutmeats. Blend well. Pour mixture into a 1½-quart mold, filling ⅔ full. Cover tightly with a lid or aluminum foil.

Place mold in a covered roasting pan. Fill roasting pan ¼ full with water. Steam the pudding in the oven at 350° for 2½ hours. Check periodically to make sure the water has not evaporated. When cool, unmold. Pudding will keep extremely well if wrapped in a brandy-soaked cheesecloth and then wrapped in foil and refrigerated, or frozen. Reheat when ready to serve.

If serving this at the dinner table, unmold on a serving plate and garnish with fresh holly sprigs for a festive presentation. Serve butter sauce on the side.

Butter Sauce

2 tablespoons flour
1 cup sugar
½ cup butter, melted
boiling water

Thoroughly mix flour and sugar. Add the butter and mix. Then slowly add boiling water, enough to make a smooth sauce. Serve warm over warmed suet pudding.

Note…
This sauce can also be used on any unfrosted cake or over ice cream.

Tutti Frutti Frosting

1½ cups sugar
1 tablespoon cocoa
1 tablespoon butter
¼ cup coconut
¼ cup nuts
¼ cup raisins
½ cup milk

Combine and cook 12-15 minutes over medium heat. Cool.

2 cups

Note…
This is a wonderful topping for an ordinary cake.

Molasses Kringles

¾ cup Crisco or shortening
1 cup sugar (brown or white)
1 egg
4 tablespoons molasses
2 cups sifted flour
2 teaspoons soda
1 teaspoon cinnamon
1 teaspoon ginger
¾ teaspoon salt

Cream the shortening, sugar, egg and molasses well. Add the dry ingredients. Chill. Roll in small balls, dip in granulated sugar. Bake at 350° for 10-15 minutes.

2 dozen

Candy
Today we call them Truffles

3 pounds sweet chocolate, divided
½ pint whipping cream

Melt 2 pounds chocolate in a double boiler. Whip cream until stiff. Add melted chocolate. Blend well and place in refrigerator to set. When set, form into balls. Melt remaining pound of chocolate. Dip balls in melted chocolate and place on wax paper to set.

2 dozen

Note…
You can also roll candies in nuts or coconut.

N

Nell's Mushroom Soup

2 pounds mushrooms, cleaned
1 medium onion, chopped
2 quarts chicken broth
6 tablespoons butter
6 tablespoons flour
salt and pepper to taste
1 cup half-and-half
1 lemon, cut into eight wedges
sour cream

Add mushrooms and onions to chicken broth in medium saucepan. Heat over medium heat and cook until soft. Strain, reserving liquid.

In a blender or food processor with steel blade, chop mushroom-onion mixture into coarse pieces. In a 2½-quart saucepan, melt butter. Add flour and cook for 2 minutes. Add reserved liquid and simmer until thickened. Correct seasonings. Can be made ahead of time to this point.

When ready to serve add the half-and-half and bring just to a boil. Pour into soup bowls. Squeeze the juice from a wedge of lemon in each bowl and top with a dollop of sour cream.

8 servings

R·e·c·i·p·e·s

Nan's Three Bean Olé

1 pound ground beef
½ pound raw bacon, diced
1 large onion, chopped
1 teaspoon cumin
1 teaspoon chili powder
1 teaspoon salt
1 16-ounce can pork & beans
1 8½-ounce can lima beans
1 16-ounce can dark kidney beans
½ cup picante sauce
½ cup brown sugar
1 teaspoon vinegar

Brown ground beef, bacon and onion. Drain. Add cumin, chili powder and salt; mix and place in a 2-quart casserole. Add the pork & beans, lima beans and kidney beans.

Mix the picante sauce, brown sugar and vinegar together; pour over the beans and bake at 325º for 2 hours. Keep warm in a chafing dish. Serve with tortilla chips.

1½ quarts

Nuts & Bolts

1½ cups butter
1 tablespoon garlic salt
1 tablespoon onion salt
1 tablespoon celery salt
6 ounces pretzel sticks
1 pound salted peanuts
1 16-ounce box Chex cereal
1 7-ounce box Cheerios cereal

Melt butter in large roasting pan and add seasonings. Add pretzels, peanuts and cereal, stirring to coat. Bake at 225º for 2 hours, stirring every half hour. Serves many.

Nell's Squiggles

Cook, drain and dry homemade or purchased fettuccine. Deep-fry in small batches until lightly browned. Drain on paper towel. Salt lightly and dip in squiggle sauce.

Nell's Squiggle Sauce

2 green bell peppers, chopped
2 12-ounce jars chili sauce
1 cup catsup
scant ½ teaspoon Tabasco
4 tablespoons oil
4 tablespoons lemon juice

Combine peppers, chili sauce, catsup, Tabasco, oil and lemon juice in a medium saucepan. Bring to boil and cook for 5-10 minutes. Keeps very well in refrigerator. Recipe can be cut in half.   3 cups

Note…
This is a great snack when you have leftover cooked fettuccine.

Nuts with a Sweet Touch

3 tablespoons butter
½ pound shelled pecan halves
¾ teaspoon salt
½ teaspoon sugar

In a 10x15-inch cookie sheet with sides, melt butter in 350º oven for 1 minute. Add pecans to butter and sprinkle with salt and sugar, stirring to coat. Brown at 350º for 15-20 minutes, turning every 5 minutes.

2 cups

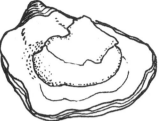

R·e·c·i·p·e·s

Oysters in Wine Sauce

A wonderful appetizer!

12 oysters in shells
white wine
white wine sauce (recipe below)
Parmesan cheese

Shuck the oysters, saving ½ of the shells. Poach the oysters in white wine to cover until edges curl; do not overcook. Place each oyster in a shell. Top with sauce and sprinkle with Parmesan cheese; pop under the broiler until lightly brownded. Place 3 on each small plate and garnish with cilantro or parsley.

4 servings

White Wine Sauce

2 cups chicken broth
2 cups white wine
1 cup whipping cream
2 cups half-and-half

In large saucepan combine broth and wine. Bring to a boil and reduce to about ¼. Add cream and half-and-half and continue to cook until reduced by ¾ or until sauce is slightly thick. Any leftover sauce can be kept in the refrigerator for 3 or 4 days, or freeze.

4 servings

Overnight Coffee Cake

2 cups flour, sifted
1 teaspoon baking powder
1 teaspoon baking soda
1 teaspoon cinnamon
½ teaspoon salt
⅔ cup margarine or butter
1 cup sugar
½ cup brown sugar, packed
2 eggs
1 cup buttermilk or 1 cup regular milk
   plus 1 teaspoon vinegar

Topping
½ cup brown sugar, packed
½ cup chopped nuts (walnuts, pecans,
   almonds or peanuts)
½ teaspoon cinnamon
¼ teaspoon nutmeg
¼ teaspoon cloves

Sift flour, baking powder, baking soda, cinnamon and salt together. Cream margarine and sugars; beat until fluffy. Add eggs one at a time, beating well. Add dry ingredients alternately with milk to creamed mixture, beating well. Spread in greased 9x13x2-inch baking pan.

For topping, combine sugar, nuts, cinnamon, nutmeg and cloves. Mix well. Sprinkle over batter. Refrigerate overnight. Bake at 350° for 45 minutes or until toothpick comes out clean.

16 servings

Orange-Spinach Salad

1 teaspoon paprika
⅔ cup sugar
1 teaspoon dry mustard
¼ teaspoon salt
⅓ cup vinegar
⅓ cup honey
1 tablespoon lemon juice
2 teaspoons grated onion
1 cup oil
1 pound spinach, washed and dried
3 oranges, peeled & sliced, cut slices in
   half
red onion rings for garnish

Blend paprika, sugar, mustard, salt, vinegar, honey, lemon juice in blender, then slowly add oil. Toss spinach and oranges in a bowl and add dressing. Garnish with red onion rings.

4-6 servings

Note…
Leftover dressing will keep well if refrigerated.

Onion Soup in Minutes

4 cups sliced onion
½ cup butter
1 49-ounce can chicken broth
½ teaspoon cayenne pepper
2 eggs
green onion for garnish

Sauté onions in butter until soft and clear. Do not brown. Place in large saucepan with chicken broth and simmer for 20 minutes; add cayenne. Beat the eggs well and add to the broth in a fine stream, stirring until all have been added. Continue to cook for 2-3 minutes. Serve garnished with chopped green onion tops.   4-6 servings

Oyster Bake

½ cup butter
¾ cup cracker crumbs
¾ cup bread crumbs
1 pint oysters, drained (reserve 2
  tablespoons liquid)
salt
pepper
2 tablespoons finely chopped onion
  or shallots
¼ cup heavy cream
¼ cup Parmesan cheese

Melt butter, add crumbs and mix. On the bottom of a 7x9-inch baking dish spread ⅓ of crumb mixture. Arrange half of the oysters on crumbs and lightly salt and pepper; add ½ the onions or shallots. Then layer another ⅓ of the crumbs, the remaining oysters, salt and pepper, and remaining onions. Combine the reserved oyster liquid and cream and pour over the layers. Add the last ⅓ of the crumbs and top with Parmesan cheese. Bake at 400° for 20-25 minutes until heated through and crumbs are slightly browned.

4 servings

Note...
Use as a side dish with fowl or fish. Can also be used as an appetizer.

Osso Bucco

6 veal shanks, 1½ to 2 inches thick
flour
5 tablespoons olive oil
3 cloves garlic
2 small onions
2 small carrots
1 rib celery
1 cup dry white wine
1 28-ounce can Italian or stewed
  tomatoes
salt and pepper

Dredge shanks in flour and brown in olive oil on all sides. Place in a small covered roasting pan. Finely chop garlic, onion, carrots and celery. Sauté in existing olive oil until soft but not brown. Add to roasting pan along with wine and tomatoes. Season with salt and pepper. Simmer for 1½ hours or until meat is well done (or oven-bake at 350°). Garnish with parsley and serve with spaetzlis.

4-6 servings

Spaetzli

3 eggs
⅓ cup water
½ teaspoon salt
2 cups flour

Beat eggs slightly. Add water and salt; mix in flour and stir well to make a smooth dough. In a large saucepan, bring water to a boil. Cut dough into small pieces on a cutting board and drop into boiling water. (Dip knife in water after each piece to keep dough from sticking.) Cook until all dumplings float to the top of the pan, then boil for 3 or 4 more minutes.   4 cups

Note...
Additions
if desired:
chives, parsley,
finely chopped onion
or a sprinkle of nutmeg.

On-Hand Chocolate Cake

This recipe is designed for immediate use or for freezing as a quick dessert. Make in three 8-inch layers or one 10x15-inch sheet cake pan.

6 eggs
1 cup sugar
1 teaspoon vanilla
½ cup flour
½ cup cocoa
⅔ cup clarified butter

Spray or grease and line the bottoms of three 8-inch tins, or grease a 10x15-inch sheet pan and dust with flour. Set aside.

Beat eggs, sugar and vanilla until very light, about 10 minutes. Sift together flour and cocoa; fold into egg mixture. Then carefully fold in butter just to combine. Divide batter into tins or pour into sheet pan. Bake at 350° for 10-12 minutes, or slightly longer for sheet pan.

For three layer cake, beat 1 cup whipping cream and spread between layers. Drained sour cherries may be added on top of whipped cream. Frost with Chocolate Ganache, (an easy chocolate frosting found on page 23) or your favorite frosting. Garnish with maraschino cherries with stems.

10-12 servings

Note...
Cut rounds of cake with a cookie cutter and use as shortcakes. Use two for each dessert, filling with fresh fruit or scoop of ice cream. Top with whipped cream, caramel or chocolate sauce. Use your imagination! This cake freezes beautifully and thaws quickly.

How to Clarify Butter

To clarify butter, cut butter into pieces and place in saucepan. Cook until bubbling, cool slightly, and pour off the clear yellow liquid. Discard the residue in the bottom of the pan.

When decorating desserts, think of seasonal touches. In spring, violets can be used on anything. They're even edible! Green mint leaves and a few berries work well in summer. For fall, try chocolate maple leaves set into whipped cream. Crushed peppermint sticks & a chocolate Santa top off a holiday dessert.

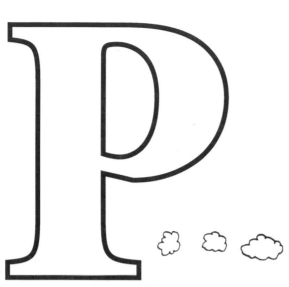

P

R·e·c·i·p·e·s

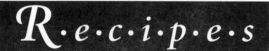

The little restaurant that could – and did!
Painted Lady, Newburg, Wisconsin
1985 - 1992
Manager and Head Chef Nell Stehr,
Owner Charlie Mayhew

Impressions:
a tasteful encounter;
Victorian parlor dining;
noontime window seat
cheese and chat –
Charlie and me;
pre-opening shenanigans
and sheepshead;
rolling pin kitchen staff persuader;
chefs need a little pâté on the back;
chocolate houses;
limousine thieves;
smart waitresses and
a dumb waiter;
tornado evacuations;
Friday night jazz;
kitchen floods;
herb garden;
labor of love;
perfection!

Mushroom Parms

45-50 mushrooms, cleaned, stems
   removed and reserved
1 cup butter, melted and divided plus
   2 tablespoons
10 green onions
2 cloves garlic
½ cup bread crumbs
1 cup ground walnuts
3 teaspoons Worcestershire sauce
⅓ teaspoon salt
1 cup Parmesan cheese

Dip mushrooms caps in 1 cup of
butter; place on cookie sheet. In
processor with steel blade process stems
with onions and garlic. Melt remaining
2 tablespoons butter in a saucepan and
sauté the onion mixture until fairly dry.
Add crumbs, nuts, Worcestershire
sauce, salt and cheese. Fill caps with
mixture until high and rounded. Bake
at 350° for 10 minutes until heated
through. Place under broiler and brown
slightly.

10-12 servings

Note…
Recipe can be cut in half. For individual
servings, place a lettuce leaf on a small
plate and arrange five mushrooms on top.

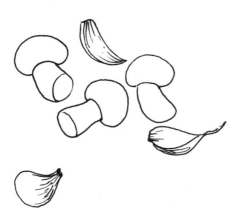

Shrimp Rosanne

¾ cup (1½ sticks) butter, softened
2 8-ounce packages cream cheese,
   softened
3 tablespoons catsup
1½ teaspoons grated onion
1½ teaspoons dill weed (optional)
6-8 fresh shrimp or 1 6-ounce can large
   shrimp, reserving 1 for garnish
parsley

Process butter, cream cheese,
catsup, onion and dill weed in food
processor until smooth. Cut shrimp
into small pieces and stir into butter
mixture. For a finer consistency process
the shrimp along with the other ingredients. Place in an attractive serving
dish. Garnish with sprinkles of
chopped parsley and 1 whole shrimp.
Serve with your favorite crackers.

2½ cups

Pepper-Onion Mayonnaise

2 tablespoons finely chopped parsley
3 tablespoons finely chopped green
   pepper
1 tablespoon finely chopped red pepper
1 tablespoon finely chopped onion
2 tablespoons finely chopped pimento
1 cup mayonnaise
⅛ teaspoon paprika
2 teaspoons lemon juice
¼ teaspoon salt
⅛ teaspoon pepper

Combine parsley, green pepper, red
pepper, onion and pimento. Add
mayonnaise, paprika, lemon juice salt
and pepper. Mix well. Add to your
favorite green salad. Toss. Extra dressing will keep well in refrigerator for
several days.　　　1½ cups

Victorian Velvet Soup

½ medium onion
2 cups chopped carrots
2 cups chopped celery
1 cup water
1 cup (2 sticks) butter
¾ cup flour
6 cups chicken broth
4 cups milk, cream or half-and-half
2¼ pounds American cheese, grated or
    cut in small pieces

Process with steel blade the onion, carrots and celery in the water until very fine. Place mixture in saucepan and add water just to cover mixture. Cook on medium heat, uncovered, until tender and most of the water has evaporated.

In a saucepan melt butter, then add flour stirring constantly for 2 minutes. Add chicken broth; bring back to boil and add milk and cheese. Continue to heat until cheese has melted. Add vegetable mixture and bring back to just a boil. If it appears too thick, add more milk or broth. To serve, garnish with finely chopped chives or green onions. Soup freezes very well.

12-16 cups

Chicken Breast Supreme

4 small chicken breasts, skinned (save
    the skins) and boned
2 cups chicken broth
2 cups white wine
1 cup whipping cream
2 cups half-and-half
White Wine Sauce recipe, page 71

Replace skin on breasts, place breasts in 9x12-inch pan and add chicken broth to cover. Cover with foil and roast until tender, about 25-30 minutes at 350°.

When chicken is tender remove and discard skin. Arrange on platter, cover with wine sauce and sprinkle with parsley. Can also be served with three cooked whole shrimp on top of each breast. Extra sauce can be served on the side.

4 servings

Breast of Quail in Puff Pastry

1¼ pounds boned quail
white wine
1 17¼-ounce package frozen puff pastry,
    thawed
 4 tablespoons plus ⅓ cup butter, divided
½ pound mushrooms, thinly sliced
½ cup diced green onions
1 teaspoon thyme, divided
5 teaspoons sesame seeds
½ teaspoon white pepper
½ teaspoon salt
⅓ cup flour
1½ cups chicken broth
2 tablespoons lemon juice
scant ½ cup cream
1 egg, beaten
2 tablespoons cream

Preheat oven to 350º. Place quail in 5x7-inch baking dish, add wine to cover meat. Cover dish and bake about 1 hour. (Cooking time varies with the age of the bird.) Chill and slice meat.

For the filling, melt 4 tablespoons butter in sauté pan. Add mushrooms and onions, sautéing until liquid has evaporated. Do not brown. Add ½ teaspoon thyme, sesame seeds, white pepper and salt; chill.

To make the sauce, melt butter; stir in flour, mixing until smooth. Cook 2 minutes. Add broth; cook until mixture thickens. Add lemon juice and remaining thyme. Add cream and bring just to a boil. If too thick add more cream. The sauce should be fairly thin.

For the glaze, combine egg with cream. Mix until smooth.

To assemble, roll puff pastry slightly with a rolling pin. Cut 4 pieces about 5x8 inches. Place equal amount of quail in the center of each pastry strip. Divide filling and place over quail.

Moisten edge of pastry with water. Fold 8-inch sides of pastry to center, then fold in the 5-inch sides and seal tightly.

Turn pastries seam-side down on a non-stick cookie sheet. Decorate tops with leftover pieces of pastry. Brush with glaze. Bake at 375º for 20-30 minutes, until golden.

Divide sauce between 4 dinner plates. Place one quail in puff pastry on each plate and garnish with strips of pimento and leaves of parsley.

4 servings

Note…
If quail is not available, alternatives are pheasant, grouse or wild turkey.

Braised Rabbit in White Wine

½ cup flour
½ teaspoon salt
½ teaspoon white pepper
½ teaspoon rosemary
1 tablespoon paprika
2 pounds rabbit, cut in pieces
¾ cup butter, divided
¾ cup white wine
1½ cups chicken broth
2 large onions, sliced

Combine flour, salt, pepper, rosemary and paprika in a plastic bag and shake to mix. Add rabbit; shake to coat. Remove rabbit; shake off excess flour.

Melt ½ cup of butter in a saucepan. Add rabbit, sautéing until golden brown. Remove meat to a baking pan just large enough to hold the pieces. Add wine to saucepan and cook until wine has been reduced by half, scraping pan to loosen any browned bits. Add broth and set aside.

Melt remaining ¼ cup butter in a sauté pan. Add onions; cook until soft and translucent but do not brown. Spoon onions over the meat and top meat with reserved wine sauce.

Preheat oven to 350º. Bake 1 hour or until meat is tender when tested with a fork.

4 servings

Shrimp Newburg

¾ cup butter, divided
½ small onion, finely chopped
¼ cup flour
2 cups milk
½ teaspoon salt
⅛ teaspoon white pepper
¾ to 1 teaspoon dill weed (optional)
1½ pounds noodles
20 large raw shrimp, peeled and cleaned

Melt ¼ cup butter in saucepan. Add onion. Sauté over low heat until onion is clear but not brown. Add flour and stir for 2 minutes. Add milk and stir constantly until thickened. Add salt, pepper and dill. Thin with additional milk if too thick. Set aside.

Cook noodles according to package directions or prepare your own. When tender, drain in a colander and set over a pan of hot water.

Sauté shrimp in remaining ½ cup butter until pink; do not overcook. Place noodles on individual dinner plates, top with sauce and arrange five shrimp per plate in decorative pattern. Garnish with sprigs of parsley.

4 servings

This book never would have happened if it weren't for the Painted Lady.

Candy Cane Pie

1 cup crushed chocolate wafers (18 wafers)
¼ cup melted butter
1 tablespoon sugar
1 quart vanilla ice cream
8 6.5-ounce candy canes, crushed, reserve ¼ cup
3 egg whites
1 cup marshmallow cream
1 teaspoon vanilla
6 ounces semisweet chocolate (or chocolate chips)
1 cup whipping cream

Mix crumbs, butter and sugar; press on bottom and sides of a 9-inch pie pan. Bake at 350° for 8 minutes. Cool.

Soften vanilla ice cream to stirring consistency and add crushed candy canes. Spoon into cooled crust. Freeze until hard.

Beat egg whites until stiff. Then beat in marshmallow cream, a large spoonful at a time. Continue beating until peaks form. Add vanilla. Spread on frozen pie, sealing to edge of crust. In a preheated 400° oven, bake pie 2-3 minutes until meringue is lightly browned. Return to freezer until ready to serve.

Just before serving, chop chocolate and put in top of a double boiler. Add cream. Heat over simmering water until chocolate melts, stirring often.

Before serving, let pie stand at room temperature about 15 minutes. Cut into wedges. Top with reserved candy canes. Pass the chocolate sauce.

6-8 servings

This dessert turned into a parfait one evening at the Painted Lady. When cut to serve, it was discovered that the ice cream was beginning to melt, so we used tall parfait glasses & spooned in the pie— crust & all! We eliminated the chocolate sauce to keep the ice cream from melting further. Instead, we added a spoon of whipped cream and sprinkled it with the reserved candy canes. People loved it and never knew we goofed!

Q

If you're concerned about fat content— look for creative ways to reduce it.

There are many good, low-fat alternatives and substitutions can be made quite successfully in most recipes.

Quiche.
Real men may
not eat it but that is their misfortune. Would
real men eat custard if they knew that it and
quiche share ninety percent of the same
(namely eggs, cream and cheese) ingredients?
Come to think of it, with all of those farm
products, quiche should be considered a
prime candidate for Wisconsin's
state food! So what if
it originated in
France?

Quenelle of Chicken Soup

2 quarts chicken broth
1 small onion, finely chopped
2 carrots, cubed
2 ribs celery, cut in small pieces
½ -¾ pounds fresh chicken breast
2 tablespoons dry bread crumbs (soften
   in small amount of milk)
2 tablespoons melted butter
1 egg slightly beaten
⅛ teaspoon cayenne pepper
½ teaspoon salt
⅛ teaspoon grated nutmeg

Combine the chicken broth, onion, carrots and celery; cook over medium heat approximately 15 minutes or until vegetables are soft. Remove from heat while making quenelles.

With a steel blade, grind or process the chicken breast until it forms a paste. Combine with bread crumbs, butter, egg, cayenne papper, salt and nutmeg. Use 2 teaspoons of mixture to form oval-shaped dumplings. Reheat broth mixture to boiling. Drop dumplings into the broth and gently boil 10 minutes or until quenelles are cooked through.

Serve soup in bowls, garnished with chopped chives and sesame seeds.

6-8 servings

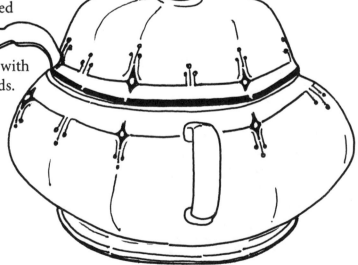

Quiche

Italian Style

pie crust for 9-inch deep pie pan
1 tablespoon olive oil
2 cups sliced zucchini
1 clove garlic, crushed
½ cup chopped onion
½ pound Italian sausage
3 eggs
1 cup milk
1 tablespoon Italian seasoning
½ teaspoon salt
4 ounces *6 Cheese Italian Blend* (mozzarella, provolone, parmesan, romano, fontina and asiago) *Available at most grocery stores.*

Line pie pan with crust. Poke holes in crust with fork and bake for 10 minutes at 350º. Set aside.

In oil, sauté the zucchini, garlic and onions until slightly cooked. Set aside. Sauté sausage until cooked through. Cool and slice in ¼ inch slices. Beat the eggs; add milk, Italian seasoning, salt and cheese. Mix.

Arrange zucchini mixture and sausage in pie crust. Pour egg mixture over filling. Bake at 350º for 30-35 minutes or until set. Let rest 5-10 minutes before serving.

6 servings

Vegetarian Style

pie crust for 9-inch deep pie pan
1 pound asparagus
1 tablespoon oil
3 tablespoons minced onion
6 ounces mushrooms
3 eggs
1 cup milk
4 ounces Swiss cheese
fresh ground pepper
½ teaspoon salt
1½ teaspoons dill weed
2 tablespoons butter

Line pie pan with crust. Poke holes in crust with fork and bake 10 minutes at 350º. Set aside.

Clean asparagus and steam for 5 minutes. Set aside.

In oil, sauté onion and mushrooms until soft but not browned. Set aside.

Beat eggs; add milk, cheese, pepper, salt and dill. Cut 3 inches off the tops of the asparagus spears and set aside. Cut the bottoms of the spears in 1-inch pieces.

Place the mushrooms and onions in the crust. Top with sliced asparagus, then arrange the reserved spears in a wagon wheel design. Dot with butter. Add egg mixture. Bake at 350º for 30-35 minutes or until lightly browned and set. Let rest 5-10 minutes before serving.

6 servingss

Note…
Broccoli also works well in this dish.

Quick Tips

- Keep flour in a shaker for easy flouring.

- Heat a knife in hot water to make a smooth job of cutting cakes.

- Grating cheese goes quicker if the grater is oiled lightly.

- Put frozen juice in a glass container, microwave for 30-40 seconds for a fast thaw.

- Rubbing your hands with parsley will remove any odor.

- Stale bread may be cut into cubes and dried thoroughly. Store in covered container. When ready to use, sauté in small amount of butter sprinkled with your favorite herbs. Cool before using on salads or soup.

- Add a sprinkle of combined sugar and cinnamon on French toast for added flavor.

- Most young people don't eat sandwich crusts. Remove crusts before assembling sandwiches. Dry them and grind for crumbs or use for stuffings.

- To doctor-up purchased spaghetti sauce, add a clove of crushed garlic, 1 teaspoon Italian herbs and ½ teaspoon oregano. Tastes more like homemade!

- Thin spaghetti sauce with vegetable juice or white wine.

- When a family member is detained, rather than keeping his or her dinner warm, make a TV-dinner and pop in microwave when he or she arrives.

- Best not to serve two creamy dishes at the same meal.

- Plan your special occasion meals ahead of time.

- As a guest, always arrive on time, but *never* early.

- Serve buffet style when entertaining a large crowd. However, for small groups a sit-down dinner is much more intimate.

- Lightly wipe a salad mold with vegetable oil; it will be much easier to unmold.

- Always preheat your oven before baking.

R

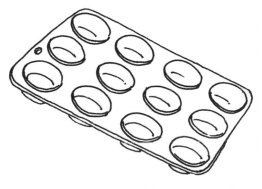

R·e·c·i·p·e·s

Renilda's Popovers

2 eggs
1 cup milk
¼ teaspoon salt
1 cup flour

In mixing bowl, beat eggs slightly. Blend in milk. Stir in salt and flour until blended. Batter may have some small lumps. To give popovers popping room, generously butter every other cup in a 12-muffin tin (5 cups) and a 6-muffin tin (3 cups). Fill cups ¾ full.

Put pans in cold oven. Turn heat to 450º and bake 20-25 minutes. Try not to open oven while popovers are baking. If oven door has window, leave oven light on and watch until popovers are deep golden brown.

Remove popovers from oven, cut slits in necks of popovers and return to oven with heat off for 10 minutes.

Serve immediately. Or, set aside and when ready to serve, reheat at 350º for 5 minutes.

8 popovers

Red Cabbage Joanne

1 head red cabbage, shredded
1 medium onion, chopped
4 strips bacon, diced
2 medium apples, chopped
1 teaspoon salt
2 tablespoons sugar
½ cup vinegar
½ cup water
1 bay leaf
pepper to taste

Put cabbage, onion, bacon, apples, salt, sugar, vinegar, water, bay leaf and pepper in a medium size saucepan. Cover and cook over low heat for 1½ hours. Stir occasionally. Remove bay leaf. Best made the day before.   6-8 servings

Rouladen

2 pounds thin round steak
3-4 tablespoons Dijon mustard
3 small onions
6 slices bacon
3 slices dark bread
⅓ cup chopped parsley
½ teaspoon marjoram
2 tablespoons capers
½ teaspoon salt
¼ teaspoon pepper
2 medium dill pickles, sliced in half
¾ cup flour
2 tablespoons oil
2 carrots
2 ribs celery
2 tablespoons butter
1 cup white or dry wine
2 cups beef broth

Pound beef until about ⅛-inch thick and cut into 4x4-inch pieces. (Should be about 8-10.) Spread each piece with mustard. Set aside.

Chop 2 of the onions and bacon into very small pieces; sauté until tender.

With steel blade process the bread along with the onion, bacon, parsley, marjoram, capers, salt and pepper. Place a dill pickle half to fit diagonally across the meat (not all the way to the edge). Spoon processed mixture on top of meat. Roll meat around filling and secure with string or toothpicks. Dredge in flour. Heat 2 tablespoons oil and brown meat on all sides. Remove to platter. Finely process the carrots, celery and remaining onion, then sauté in butter for 5 minutes in the pan in which you browned meat. Add beef rolls, wine and broth to the pan. Simmer or bake at 350° and cook until tender, about 1½ hours. Serve with spaetzli and red cabbage.

4-5 servings

Note…
Instead of cutting into the 4x4-inch pieces, you can use the single piece of meat, proceeding in exactly the same way. Slice when ready to serve.

Rolls with a Twist

1¼-ounce package dry yeast
1½ cups warm milk or water (105-115°)
½ cup sugar
½ cup vegetable oil
1 teaspoon salt
4-5 cups flour
sesame seed or poppy seeds

Dissolve yeast in ½ cup warm milk; let stand 5 minutes. In large bowl combine yeast mixture, remaining milk, sugar, oil, salt and half the flour. Beat on low speed until smooth. Stir in remaining flour to make a soft dough. Knead until smooth and elastic, 8-10 minutes. Place in greased bowl; let rise until doubled. Shape dough into "S", Pretzel or Crescent shapes. Let rise again until doubled. Sprinkle with sesame or poppy seeds. Bake at 375° for 15-20 minutes or until nicely browned.

1 dozen

Note...
Some additions to dough:
    1 cup grated cheese
    1 cup candied orange peel
    1 cup chopped raisins or dates
    1 cup fried and crumbled bacon

"S" Shape

Roll portions of dough in 9-inch ropes about 1-inch thick. Shape into "S" shape.

Pretzel Shape

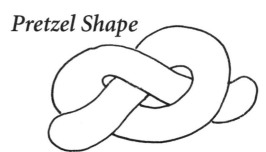

Roll dough into long ropes ½-inch in diameter, 8-inches long. Carefully tie each rope into a loose knot.

Crescent Shape

Roll a portion of dough into a 12-inch circle. Cut into 12 wedges. Roll lightly, beginning at the wide end, sealing end with a drop of water. Shape into a half moon.

Note...
Another tasty treat is to spread the crescent-cut dough with melted butter and cinnamon sugar before rolling. Or spread with favorite jam.

Raspberry René Cheesecake

1½ cups chocolate wafers, crushed
¼ cup melted butter
2½ pounds cream cheese, softened
2 cups sugar
5 eggs
scant ½ cup Raspberry Liqueur
6 ounces semi-sweet chocolate
¾ cup sour cream

Combine wafers and butter and press into 10-inch springform pan.

Beat cheese until light. Add sugar and beat well. Add the eggs, one at a time; add the liqueur. Bake at 300° for 1 hour or until set. Turn off oven and let cake rest in oven for 1 hour.

Melt chocolate and sour cream. Blend thoroughly. Frost cheesecake when cold, and top with fresh raspberries.

12-14 servings

Raspberry Sauce
This is a very simple recipe.

2 10-ounce packages frozen raspberries, thawed
½ tablespoon lemon juice
sugar

Puree berries in a blender; add lemon juice. Strain through a fine sieve. Add sugar to taste.

Uses:
Topping for ice cream sundaes, fruit crepes, chocolate, shortcakes, fresh fruit or plain cheesecake.

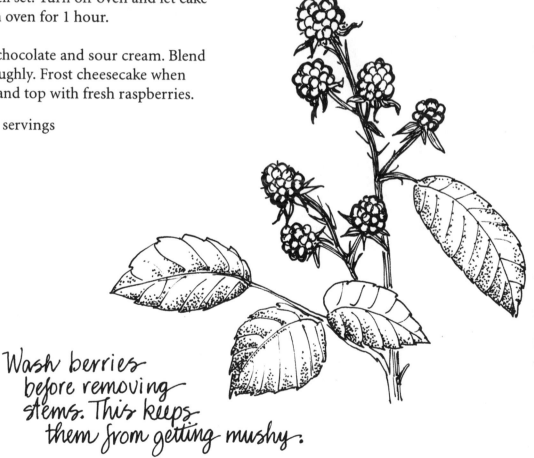

Wash berries before removing stems. This keeps them from getting mushy.

S

R·e·c·i·p·e·s

Spam Broiled Sandwiches
Before you turn up your nose, try them!

> 1 12-ounce can Spam
> 6 hard boiled eggs
> 1 16-ounce box Velveeta Cheese
> 1 small onion
> 12 buns, split

Put Spam, eggs, cheese and onion through grinder or combine in food processor. Spread on buns and broil until bubbly and lightly browned.

24 split buns

Note...
Ham may be substituted.

Dijon Dressing

⅓ cup Dijon mustard
1 tablespoon salt
1½ cups lemon juice
2 cups olive oil
2 cups salad oil

Combine mustard, salt, lemon juice, olive oil and salad oil until thoroughly blended. Keep well- refrigerated.

6 cups

Garlic Dressing

2 green onions, tops included
4 tablespoons parsley leaves
3 cloves garlic
1 cup mayonnaise
1 cup sour cream
salt
pepper

With steel blade, process onions, parsley and garlic until very fine. Add to mayonnaise and sour cream. Salt and pepper to taste.

2 cups

Note…
For a variation, add 2 teaspoons cracked pepper.

Basil Dressing

1 cup salad oil
1 cup olive oil
¼ cup sugar
½ cup red wine vinegar
1 teaspoon basil
1 teaspoon Italian seasoning
salt to taste

Mix salad oil, olive oil, sugar, wine vinegar, basil, Italian seasoning and salt together. Whisk well before using.

2½ cups

Summer Vegetable Plate

2 quarts water
8 ounces homemade or packaged noodles
1 teaspoon salt
1 cup fresh yellow beans, cut into 1-inch lengths
1 cup fresh green beans, cut into 1-inch lengths
1 cup unpeeled zucchini sliced into ¼ inch rounds
1 cup small broccoli flowerets
1 cup green pepper, julienne strips
½ cup red pepper, julienne strips
1 cup patty pan squash, sliced
2 tablespoons olive oil
1 tablespoon plus ¼ cup butter, divided
¼ cup green onions, chopped
1 clove garlic, crushed
½ cup chopped parsley
2 jalapeño peppers, seeded and finely chopped
½ teaspoon crushed pepper flakes
½ cup fresh or 2 teaspoons dried basil leaves
1 cup Chinese pea pods
½ cup chicken stock
½ cup white wine
½ cup freshly grated Parmesan cheese
½ cup salted sunflower seeds

In a large saucepan bring 2 quarts water and the salt to a boil, add noodles and cook according to package directions. (If using the homemade noodles, boil for 3 minutes.) Drain and set aside.

Blanch beans, zucchini, broccoli, peppers and squash in additional boiling water until tender. Drain and chill in cold water. Drain. Set aside.

Heat olive oil and 1 tablespoon butter in a large skillet over medium heat. Add green onions, garlic, parsley and jalapeño peppers. Sauté 2 or 3 minutes; do not brown. Add crushed pepper flakes, basil and Chinese pea pods; continue cooking until pea pods are slightly cooked, another 2 minutes. Add the blanched vegetables. Turn off heat. In a saucepan combine remaining ¼ cup butter, chicken broth and white wine. Bring to a boil and add cooked noodles, stirring until well-heated. Reheat the vegetables. Divide the noodles on to four dinner plates. Arrange the vegetable medley on the noodles. Garnish with Parmesan cheese and sunflower seeds.

4 generous servings, 6 smaller

Note...
If all the fresh vegetables are not available, frozen can be substituted.
A good crusty garlic bread is all you need to make this a complete meal.

Scalloped Carrots

12 medium carrots, peeled and sliced
1 small onion, minced
¼ cup butter
¼ cup flour
1 teaspoon salt
¼ teaspoon dry mustard
2 cups milk
¼ teaspoon celery salt
⅛ teaspoon pepper
½ pound sharp American cheese slices, divided
2 cups buttered bread crumbs (see below)

Cook carrots until tender; drain. In a medium saucepan, sauté onion in butter 2-3 minutes. Stir in flour, salt, mustard and milk. Cook, stirring until smooth. Add celery salt and pepper.

In a 2-quart casserole arrange layer of carrots then layer of cheese. Repeat until both are used up, ending with the carrots.

Pour sauce over top and sprinkle with buttered crumbs. Bake uncovered in preheated, 350° oven about 25 minutes or until well-heated and crumbs are golden.

10 servings

Note...
This can be prepared ahead, refrigerated and baked later. If cold, allow 10-15 minutes longer for baking. Ideal for company or potluck suppers.

Sopapillas

2 cups flour
1 teaspoon salt
1 teaspoon baking powder
1½ teaspoons oil
¼ cup milk
½ cup lukewarm water

Sift flour, salt and baking powder together. Add oil and work in with fingers. Add milk and water and knead until dough feels like the lobe of your ear. Let rest 15 minutes or longer.

Roll dough into a rectangle ⅛-inch thick and carefully cut into 3-inch squares. (Re-rolling dough is impossible.)

Drop in hot oil (375-400°), submerging each piece with a spoon until it begins to puff. Cook until brown on one side; turn and brown on other side.

Traditionally a corner is torn off and the sopapilla is filled with honey.

12 sopapillas

Buttered Crumbs

½ cup butter
2 cups fresh bread crumbs

Melt butter, add crumbs and mix.

Strata Ham and Mushroom

12 slices bread, crusts removed
6 slices ham
10 ounces mushrooms, sliced
¼ cup chopped onion
6 eggs, beaten
3⅓ cups milk
1 teaspoon dry mustard
12 ounces cheddar cheese

In a buttered 9x13x2-inch dish arrange 6 slices of bread. Top each slice with ham, mushrooms, chopped onion, and the last 6 slices of bread.

Beat eggs, milk and mustard. Pour over the bread. Top with the cheese. Cover and refrigerate overnight. Remove and let rest 25 minutes. Bake uncovered for 55-60 minutes at 325°.

6 servings

Note...
I would recommend starting in a cold oven. Moisture on a glass dish can cause it to crack on contact with a hot oven rack.

Some variations that can be used are:
* ham and broccoli*
* sausage and mushrooms*
* broccoli and mushrooms*
* asparagus and mushrooms*
* asparagus and ham, sausage or bacon*

Combine things the family enjoys!

Shrimp-Rice Casserole

1 large onion, chopped
1 tablespoon butter
1 10¾-ounce can cream of mushroom soup
1 10¾-ounce can cream of celery soup
1 tablespoon lemon juice
dash garlic salt
2 cups cooked rice
1 6-ounce can shrimp or crab meat, or mixture of both
1 cup sour cream
1 cup shredded cheddar cheese

Heat butter in large saucepan and sauté onion until translucent. Add soups, lemon juice and garlic salt. Fold in rice and shrimp. Add sour cream and pour into a 2-quart casserole. Sprinkle with cheese. Bake uncovered at 325° for 30 minutes. If dish has been refrigerated bake at 350° for 45 minutes.

Green pepper rings can be added to top for garnish.

4 servings

Southern Pecan Cheesecake

This is a rich, delicious dessert that goes a long way. Simple to prepare, this cheesecake is a welcomed addition to holiday entertaining.

1½ cups graham crackers
2 tablespoons sugar
¼ cup plus 2 tablespoons melted butter
2½ pounds cream cheese, room temperature
1⅔ cups brown sugar
5 eggs
1 teaspoon vanilla
1 cup chopped pecans

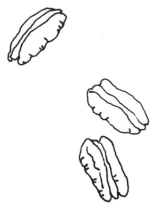

Combine graham crackers, sugar and melted butter; press onto the bottom of a 10-inch springform pan.

Beat the cream cheese, brown sugar, eggs and vanilla until very creamy using an electric mixer on medium speed. Add the chopped nuts and pour into the crust. Bake at 325º for 1 hour or until set. Turn off the oven. Leave the cheesecake in the oven for an additional half hour.

Cool at room temperature then refrigerate for at least 8 hours or overnight. Ideal when made a day ahead.

When cool, cover the top with whipped cream and garnish the edges with additional chopped pecans.

14-16 servings

T

Tea Sandwiches in Bread Basket

1 large loaf unsliced bread cut to form a basket with handle.

Use a variety of breads: white, wheat and grain. Trim crusts to form a square.

Fill each sandwich with the same filling or be creative and use several. Some suggestions: egg salad; ham salad; chicken salad; thin-sliced tomatoes, lightly sprinkled with Italian seasoning and mayonnaise; softened cream cheese combined with chopped ripe or green olives, chopped pickles, watercress sprigs, pecans or walnuts, chopped dates, etc.

When sandwiches are filled, cut into 4 triangular pieces and "fill" your basket. For an authentic "tea," serve iced tea and side dishes of carrot and celery sticks, small gherkin pickles and stuffed olives. For dessert serve small pieces of almond layer cookies.

Toasted Crab on Bun

1 6½-ounce can crab meat
¾ cup mayonnaise
1 cup grated sharp cheddar cheese
⅓ tablespoon curry
pinch salt
½ onion, finely chopped
⅓ cup green pepper, finely chopped
1 teaspoon Worcestershire sauce
dash *Accent*
8 sesame seed buns

Combine crab, mayonnaise, cheese, curry, salt, onion, green pepper, Worcestershire sauce and *Accent*. Mix well. Split 8 buns creating 16 halves; spread each half with mixture. Broil 12-15 minutes, placing pan 8-inches from the broiler.

8 servings

Tasty Crab Dip

1 8-ounce package cream cheese, softened
1 tablespoon finely grated onion
1 tablespoon dill weed
½ cup sour cream
2 tablespoons mayonnaise
dash or two Tabasco sauce
1 6-ounce can white crab meat

Combine cream cheese, onion, dill weed, sour cream, mayonnaise and Tabasco. Mix thoroughly. Add crab and gently mix. Can be garnished with strips of pimento and sliced black olives.

Serve with fresh vegetables and your favorite chips.

2 cups

Tomatoes Broiled with Herbs

4 tablespoons butter
¾ cup bread crumbs
½ teaspoon garlic salt
1 teaspoon basil
8 ½-inch slices of tomato

Melt butter. Add crumbs, garlic salt and basil. Spread on tomato slices. Broil 8 inches away from flame for 5-7 minutes or until lightly browned.

4 servings

Touch of Italy Chicken

4 chicken breasts, skinned and boned
Italian seasoning
salt and pepper
½ package (10-ounce) fresh spinach, cooked and drained
provolone cheese
4 teaspoons plus ½ cup (1 stick) butter, divided
2 eggs
2½ cups bread crumbs
1 teaspoon Italian seasoning
1 teaspoon paprika

Wash chicken breasts; place between wax paper and pound thin. Sprinkle breasts with Italian seasoning, salt and pepper. Place ¼ of spinach down the center of each breast. Top with a finger of provolone cheese. Top with 1 teaspoon butter. Fold chicken like an envelope, encasing spinach, cheese and butter.

Beat eggs. Combine bread crumbs, Italian seasoning and paprika and mix well. Dip chicken in egg, then in bread crumbs, holding so envelopes don't unfold. Let dry in refrigerator for 15 minutes then re-dip in egg and crumbs. (You can bake at this time or hold them in the refrigerator for several hours.) When ready to bake, melt the stick of butter and roll the chicken in the butter, turning to coat. Place in a shallow baking dish and pour any remaining butter over the chicken. Bake at 375º for 25-30 minutes, turning once. Make a small cut in the chicken to check for doneness (no pink!).

4 servings

Note…
Serve with Gourmet Wild Rice, page 33, and Tomatoes Broiled with Herbs, page 96.

Turkey-Asparagus Lasagna

2 tablespoons plus ⅓ cup butter, divided
1 pound freshly ground turkey
½ cup chopped green pepper
1 clove garlic, chopped
6 ounces mushrooms
⅓ cup chopped onions
½ cup chopped celery
1½ teaspoons thyme, divided
½ teaspoon salt
¼ teaspoon pepper
⅓ cup butter
⅓ cup flour
3 cups milk
9 lasagna noodles, cooked and set aside
1 pound fresh asparagus, cooked and set aside
1½ cups shredded Monterey jack cheese
1½ cups shredded Parmesan cheese

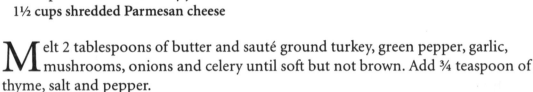

Melt 2 tablespoons of butter and sauté ground turkey, green pepper, garlic, mushrooms, onions and celery until soft but not brown. Add ¾ teaspoon of thyme, salt and pepper.

In a separate saucepan, melt remaining ⅓ cup butter; add flour and cook for 2 minutes. Add remaining ½ teaspoon thyme and milk; bring to a boil. Cook until thick. If too thick, thin with additional milk. Salt and pepper to taste.

To assemble, put a small amount of sauce on the bottom of a lightly-buttered 9x13-inch casserole. Arrange 3 lasagna noodles over sauce; divide the turkey mixture and spread half of it over the noodles. Cut asparagus spears in half; layer half of the asparagus over the turkey mixture. Add ⅓ of the remaining sauce, cover with ⅓ of each of the cheeses. Repeat with a second layer of noodles, turkey, asparagus, ⅓ of sauce and ⅓ of the cheeses. Top with last 3 lasagna noodles and cover with the remaining ⅓ sauce and the remaining cheeses. Bake at 350° for 30 minutes or until golden brown and bubbly.

4-6 servings

Note...
This dish is equally tasty using broccoli instead of asparagus.

U

Under no circumstances...
Frosted Creams

Under no circumstances use this recipe for Frosted Creams. This is an old recipe I acquired from three different relatives, not one of whom could remember ever using it. I followed the recipe as written – baking, frosting, cutting into squares. They turned out as hard as rocks! So, if you cherish your teeth, dunk them in coffee, milk or tea. However, the flavor is not too bad!

1 cup butter or margarine, softened
1 cup sugar
1 cup molasses
1 tablespoon soda in a little water
1 tablespoon cinnamon
1 teaspoon ginger
1 teaspoon baking powder
5½ cups flour
1 cup hot water
2 tablespoons butter, softened
1½ cups confectioners' sugar
1½ tablespoons milk
½ teaspoon vanilla

Cream butter with sugar. Add molasses and soda. Sift cinnamon, ginger, baking powder and flour. Add flour mixture and water alternately to sugar mixture. Pour in greased 9x12-inch pan. Bake at 350º for 40 minutes or until toothpick comes out clean. Cut in squares and frost while hot.

For frosting, blend butter and ½ cup of sugar, then add remaining sugar, milk and vanilla. Blend well.

Note:
Can add 1 cup raisins or chopped pecans or a combination.

Updating a Shrimp Cocktail

white bread
2 tablespoons butter
¼ teaspoon garlic salt
1 cup catsup
1 tablespoon lemon juice
1 tablespoon horseradish or to taste
¼ cup very finely chopped celery
12 large shrimp, cleaned and cooked

Cut 12, two-inch round or diamond-shaped pieces of white bread. Cut a round or triangle in the middle of each piece and discard center. Combine butter and garlic salt and lightly sauté bread shapes until lightly browned. Cool.

Mix catsup, lemon juice, horseradish and celery together.

When ready to serve, stand a shrimp in the middle of each piece of bread. Place three on each plate, and on the side add a spoonful of the sauce. Garnish with a sprig of parsley.

4 servings

Unconventional Onions

5 tablespoons butter
4 medium onions, thinly sliced
2 tablespoons sugar

Melt butter in a large skillet. Add the sliced onions and cook until translucent. Add sugar stirring often until onions are deep golden brown and caramelized, 15-20 minutes.

Note…
Suggested uses are as a topping for your favorite hamburger, pork chops, fish, baked or mashed potatoes or lamb patties. These are wonderful alternatives to the conventional fried onions!

By the Author

Ultimate Omelet

1 6-ounce can white crab meat
½ pound shrimp, cooked and cleaned, cut in small pieces
½ cup slivered almonds, toasted
½ cup mayonnaise
¼ cup sour cream
1 tablespoon lemon juice
1 teaspoon salt, divided
1½ teaspoons dill weed, divided
1 10¾-ounce can cream of shrimp soup
¾ cup half-and-half
¼ cup butter
½ cup flour
dash cayenne
2 cups milk
4 eggs, separated

Note...
A great luncheon dish! Then back to the bridge table...

Drain crab. Combine crab, shrimp, almonds, mayonnaise, sour cream, lemon juice, ½ teaspoon of salt and ½ teaspoon of dill weed. Set aside until omelet is baked.

Dilute the soup with half-and-half. Add remaining ¾ teaspoon dill weed. Set aside.

Grease 15x10x2-inch jelly roll pan; line with wax paper; oil paper; dust with flour. Set aside.

To make omelet, melt butter in medium saucepan. Blend in flour, remaining ½ teaspoon salt and cayenne. Slowly stir in milk and keep stirring until mixture is thick. Boil 1 minute. Remove from heat.

Beat egg whites until soft peaks form. Set aside. Beat egg yolks, then very slowly add to hot milk mixture. Fold in egg whites just until blended. Spread evenly into jelly roll pan. Bake at 325° for 40-45 minutes or until golden brown and the top springs back when lightly pressed with fingertips. Run a knife around edges of pan and cover omelet with wax paper or foil. Place a large cookie sheet or tray on top. Quickly turn upside down. Lift pan and peel wax paper off.

Heat crab salad mixture just until warmed and spread on omelet. Roll omelet jelly roll fashion. Put on decorative tray or large plate.

Heat soup mixture and place a portion on the omelet; serve remaining soup mixture on the side. Garnish with sprigs of parsley.

6 servings

Unique Uses for Puff Pastry

Puff pastry can be used with many food dishes. It is easy to find in the frozen food section of your food store. You can make your own but the purchased pastry is equally good. I recommend it.

Chicken in Puff Pastry

3 slices day-old bread
¼ cup chopped onions
6 mushrooms, sliced
1 rib celery, finely chopped
3 tablespoons plus 1 teaspoon butter, divided
½ teaspoon salt
¼ teaspoon pepper
¾ teaspoon poultry seasoning or thyme
1 17¼-ounce package (2 sheets) frozen Puff Pastry, defrosted
2 large chicken breasts poached in chicken broth, boned and sliced *or* 3 cups leftover chicken, sliced
1 egg
1 teaspoon water
3 tablespoons butter
3 tablespoons flour
½ teaspoon salt
⅛ teaspoon pepper
¾ teaspoon thyme
3 cups chicken broth

Soak the bread in small amount of water to soften; press excess water out. Sauté onions, mushrooms and celery in 2 tablespoons of butter until soft and fairly dry. Mix with the bread; add salt, pepper and poultry seasoning.

To assemble, cut puff pastry into four, 6x8-inch pieces, trimming corners to make an oval. In the middle of each piece of pastry, place ¼ of the bread mixture. Top with slices of chicken. Add 1 teaspoon remaining butter to each. Moisten edges with water, fold pastry to cover the chicken forming a square. Place on a cookie sheet seam side down. On top, in the middle of the square, make a small hole to let steam escape. Use leftover pastry to decorate top. Beat egg and water to make glaze. Brush over pastry. Bake at 350° for 25 minutes or until pastry is puffed and evenly browned.

To make sauce, melt butter and flour, cook 2 minutes. Add salt, pepper, thyme and chicken broth. Bring to boil and simmer for a few minutes. Serve on side of pastries.

4 servings

Seafood in Puff Pastry

1 17¼-ounce package frozen Puff Pastry, defrosted
1 pound cod fish
white wine
2 tablespoons plus ¼ cup butter, divided
2 ribs celery, chopped
½ cup chopped onion
3 slices bread
1 teaspoon dill weed
1 teaspoon salt, divided
¼ teaspoon pepper
12 medium shrimp
¼ cup flour
2 cups canned clam juice
⅛ teaspoon white pepper
½ cup fresh lemon juice
1½ teaspoons dill weed (optional)
1 egg, beaten
1 teaspoon water

In saucepan, place cod in a single layer, cover with white wine and poach about 10-15 minutes or until fish flakes. Remove from wine. (If fish falls apart, strain. Fish does not have to remain intact.)

Melt 2 tablespoons of butter; sauté celery and onions until soft and clear. Soak bread in water to soften and squeeze out excess water and place in a bowl. Add sautéed onion and celery, dillweed, ½ teaspoon of salt and pepper.

Clean shrimp and remove shell, cleaning back of shrimp. Sauté in 4 tablespoons butter but do not brown.

Melt remaining ¼ cup butter, add flour and cook 2 minutes. Add clam juice, remaining ½ teaspoon salt and white pepper. Bring to a boil and simmer 5 minutes. Add lemon juice and dill weed, if desired.

To assemble, cut puff pastry into four, 6x8-inch pieces. Trim corners to make oval. In the middle of each, place ¼ of dressing, top with ¼ of the flaked fish, then top off with 3 shrimp. Moisten pastry with water and fold to make a square. Place on cookie sheet seam-side down. Decorate top with extra pastry. Make a vent on top with the point of knife.

Beat together egg and water to make a glaze. Brush over pastry. Bake at 350° for 25 minutes or until pastry is puffed and brown.

4 servings

Apple Dumplings in Puff Pastry

¼ cup brown sugar
1 teaspoon cinnamon
¼ teaspoon nutmeg
¼ teaspoon ground cloves
4 teaspoons butter, softened
1 17¼-ounce package Puff Pastry,
   defrosted
4 large tart apples, peeled and cored
1 egg
1 teaspoon water

Combine brown sugar, cinnamon, nutmeg, cloves and butter. Mix well.

Bring puff pastry to room temperature. Cut small round to fit the bottom of each apple. Then cut strips ½-inch wide and moisten with water; wrap strips around apple, leaving cored area open. Fill opening with sugar mixture. Continue to cover with pastry, leaving small area open so steam can escape. Decorate top with leaves cut out of pastry scraps. Beat egg and water to make glaze. Carefully brush pastry with glaze. Bake at 350º for 25 minutes or until nicely browned and apples are tender. Serve with Hot Caramel Rum Sauce or ice cream.

Hot Caramel Rum Sauce

1 12-ounce jar caramel topping
2 tablespoons butter
1 ½ ounces dark rum

Heat ingredients together, serve over apple.

4 servings

Note…
Pie crust can also be used instead of puff pastry. This recipe works equally well with pears.

Vegetable Summer Lasagna

2 tablespoons oil
½ small eggplant, cubed
1 medium zucchini, cubed
½ medium onion, chopped
½ cup chopped green pepper
4 ounces sliced fresh mushrooms
¾ cup celery, diced
1 carrot, diced
2 16-ounce cans stewed tomatoes
1 teaspoon Italian seasoning
1 teaspoon basil
½ teaspoon salt
¼ teaspoon pepper
9 lasagna noodles
1 cup cottage cheese, small curd
1 cup grated Parmesan cheese,
1 cup shredded mozzarella cheese

In a saucepan, heat oil and sauté eggplant, zucchini, onion, green pepper, mushroom, celery and carrots until soft. Add tomatoes, Italian seasoning, basil, salt and pepper. Cover and simmer for 10 minutes. Cook lasagna in salted water as per package directions.

Spread ¼ of the sauce in a lightly greased 13x9x2-inch pan. Arrange 3 noodles over the sauce. Top with ⅓ of the cottage cheese, ¼ of the Parmesan and mozzarella cheeses, and ¼ of the sauce mixture. Repeat layers two more times. Top with remaining cheese. Bake uncovered at 350° for 30-40 minutes.

4-6 servings

Variations on a Muffin

Basic Sweet Batter
 ½ cup butter
 1 cup sugar
 2 eggs
 3 cups flour
 3 teaspoons baking powder
 pinch soda
 ½ teaspoon salt
 1 cup milk
 1 teaspoon vanilla

Cream butter and sugar. Add eggs, one at a time, mixing after each addition. Combine flour, baking powder, soda and salt. Add the flour mixture alternately with the milk to creamed mixture. Mix thoroughly. Add your choice of variations. If using one or two variations, use 1 cup of each. If using 3 or more variations, use only ½ cup of each.

Variations or Combinations
 Add to batter any of the following:
 1 cup chopped apples
 1 cup raisins (soften in a little warm water)
 1 cup drained crushed pineapple
 1 cup finely grated carrots
 1 cup pecans
 1 cup coconut
 1 cup blueberries
 1 cup sour cherries
 1 cup fresh cranberries
 1 cup dates

Spices
 Add spices you like or a combination of all:
 1 teaspoon cinnamon
 ½ teaspoon nutmeg
 ¼ teaspoon ground cloves
 ½ teaspoon almond extract
 1 teaspoon vanilla

Streusel Topping
 ½ cup flour
 ½ cup brown sugar
 ¼ cup butter
Combine flour and sugar. Cut in butter until well-mixed. Sprinkle on top of muffins before baking.

Other Toppings
 Plain sugar
 Brown sugar
 Nuts

 12-18 muffins

Veal Milan

1 16-ounce can tomato sauce
3 teaspoons Italian seasoning, divided
1 clove garlic, chopped
¾ teaspoon salt
½ teaspoon pepper
1-1½ cups bread crumbs
4-6 ounces veal scallopini, pounded thin
2 medium eggs, beaten well
2 tablespoons oil or butter
4 large slices mozzarella cheese

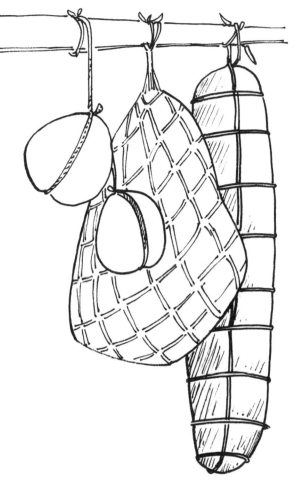

Heat the tomato sauce, 2 teaspoons of Italian seasoning and garlic and simmer for 10 minutes. Keep warm.

Mix remaining 1 teaspoon Italian seasoning, salt and pepper into bread crumbs. Dip the pounded veal into egg then in crumbs. Sauté on medium heat in olive oil or butter until browned and cooked through, 7-10 minutes.

Place slices of veal in a 7x11-inch shallow dish, cover with sauce and top with slices of mozzarella cheese. Pop under broiler until cheese is melted and lightly browned. Serve with snap peas and Italian bread.

4 servings

Vegetable Casserole

    4 long carrots, cut in strips
    3 stalks celery, chunked
    1 medium onion, diced
    1 green pepper, cut in strips
    2 10-ounce packages frozen green beans
    3 tomatoes, chopped
    2 tablespoons sugar
    2 tablespoons butter
    2 tablespoons minute tapioca
    salt and pepper

Mix carrots, celery, onion, green pepper, green beans, tomatoes, sugar, butter, tapioca, salt and pepper together and put in 2-quart casserole. Cover and bake at 300º for 2 hours.

12 servings

Vegetable Casserole No. 2

    2 green peppers, sliced into thin strips
    1 red pepper, sliced into thin strips
    1½ cups whipping cream
    1½ cups mayonnaise
    ⅔ cup grated cheddar cheese
    salt and pepper
    1 10-ounce box frozen peas, thawed
    1 10-ounce box lima beans, thawed
    1 10-ouncebox French green beans,
       thawed

Blanch peppers in small amount of boiling water for 2 minutes. Drain.

Mix whipping cream, mayonnaise, cheese, salt and pepper together to form a sauce.

Butter a large casserole. Add peppers, peas and beans and cover with sauce. Bake uncovered at 325º for 45-50 minutes until light brown and puffed.

10 servings

W

R·e·c·i·p·e·s

Venison in Wine Sauce

3 tablespoons cooking oil
2 tablespoons butter
4 pounds venison, cut in 2-inch by ½-inch strips
1 teaspoon salt
¼ teaspoon pepper
1 bay leaf
¼ cup minced parsley
3 cups chicken broth
1 cup dry red wine
1 10-ounce can pearl onions, undrained
1 pound fresh mushrooms, sliced
2-4 tablespoons cornstarch
½ cup water
hot buttered noodles

In Dutch oven or heavy pan melt butter and oil. Sauté venison strips a few at a time; don't crowd. Remove strips as they brown.

Return all browned venison to Dutch oven and add salt, pepper, bay leaf and parsley. Stir in broth and wine. Cover and simmer on low heat about 1 hour. Add onions with juice and mushrooms. Simmer, covered, another ½ hour or until meat is tender.

When meat is tender, mix cornstarch with water, stir into venison mixture and simmer about 3 minutes more to thicken. Serve with buttered noodles on the side.

12 servings

White Bread, Martin

2 ounces compressed yeast
4½ cups warm water (110°)
1 tablespoon salt
⅓ cup lard
2 teaspoons sugar
12 cups flour

Dissolve yeast in water; add salt, lard and sugar. Add flour until barely sticky. Knead until very smooth and elastic.

Warm a large, well-greased bowl and add dough and cover. Let dough rise in a draft-free area until doubled in bulk, about 1½ hours. Punch down and let rise again. Punch down and divide into four, 9x5x3-inch loaf pans. Let rise until about 2-inches above the pan. Bake at 350° in a gas oven, 375° in an electric oven for 25 minutes. Turn loaves over in the pans and bake another 35 minutes or until golden brown.

4 loaves

This recipe is from Martin Chesak. As of this printing, he is 88 and still making bread for himself and his children.

Wild Rice and Portabella Mushroom Soup

⅓ cup butter
¾ cup minced onions
2 cups chopped portabella mushrooms
½ cup flour
3 cups chicken stock
2½ cups cooked wild rice
salt and pepper to taste
1½ cups heavy cream
¾ cup dry wine (optional)

In a large pan melt butter. Add onions and mushrooms and sauté until soft. Add flour, stirring constantly for 2 minutes. Add chicken broth and stir, mixing well. Add rice and simmer for 20 minutes. Salt and pepper to taste. Blend in cream and wine and heat to just a boil.

6-8 servings

Note…
If soup appears to be too thick, add additional chicken stock. Other varieties of mushrooms will work as well.

A slice of the mushroom which has been sautéed in a small amount of butter makes a nice garnish. Sprinkle with the zest of a lemon.

Wild Game Sauce

½ cup currant jelly
¼ cup port wine
¼ cup catsup
½-1 teaspoon Worcestershire sauce
2 tablespoons butter.

Mix jelly, wine, catsup, Worcestershire sauce and butter together. Heat and serve.

1 cup

Note…
This sauce can be served on the side with any game meat. Also very good on pork or domestic duck.

Ken would provide everything but the noodles.

Turtle Soup

    4 quarts turtle stock (recipe follows)
    1 quart tomato juice
    1 large onion, finely diced
    4 large carrots, finely diced
    3 ribs celery, finely diced
    3 medium potatoes, finely diced
    1 10-ounce package frozen cut green beans or 1 16-ounce can cut green beans, drained
    turtle meat (from stock)
    knopfli (recipe follows)

Heat stock in large kettle or Dutch oven. Add tomato juice, onion, carrots, celery, potatoes and beans. Simmer covered about 1 hour or until vegetables are tender.

Meanwhile, thoroughly wash scum off turtle meat, remove meat from bones and dice into small pieces.

When vegetables are cooked, prepare knopfli dough. To add knopfli to boiling soup, take a teaspoonful of dough and using another teaspoon, slice off small pieces into the soup. (Dip spoons in soup frequently to prevent sticking.) Boil knopflis briskly another 5 minutes. Add turtle meat; adjust seasonings and heat through.

12-15 servings

Note...
Make soup a day ahead to give flavors a chance to blend.

Turtle Stock

    4 pounds turtle meat, on bones with fat removed (snappers)
    4 quarts water
    1 tablespoon salt
    1 teaspoon pepper
    2 carrots, cut into coarse pieces
    2 ribs celery, cut into coarse pieces
    1 medium onion, cut into coarse pieces

Put turtle meat into large kettle or Dutch oven; add water. Bring to boil; skim. Add salt, pepper, carrots, celery and onion. Cover and simmer for 2 ½ hours. Remove turtle meat; set aside. Strain broth through fine sieve. Discard vegetables.

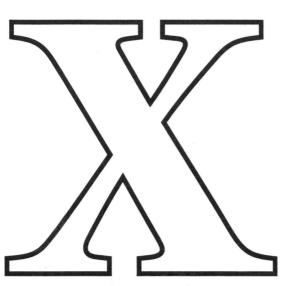

X

Xnipec
Yucatan Salsa

> 2 medium tomatoes
> 1 medium onion
> 12 sprigs fresh cilantro
> 6 seraglio chilies
> 6 tablespoons orange juice
> 3 tablespoons grapefruit juice
> 2 tablespoons lemon juice
> 1 teaspoon salt

Dice tomatoes, onion, cilantro and chilies. Set aside. Mix orange juice, grapefruit juice, lemon juice and salt together. Combine all ingredients. Serve with your choice of crackers or tortilla chips.

1 cup

Note...
This can also be used as a topping for tacos.

X-Rated Gershwin Torte

1 cup flour, sifted
1 teaspoon baking powder
6 eggs, separated, room temperature
6 tablespoons plus ⅓ cup sugar, divided
1 teaspoon vanilla
2 tablespoons butter, melted
Frosting and Nut Brittle (recipe follows)

Sift flour and baking powder. Set aside. Beat egg yolks and 6 table-spoons of sugar until light and lemon-colored. Add vanilla. In a separate bowl, beat egg whites until soft peaks form. Gradually add remaining ⅓ cup sugar, beating until stiff.

Add ¼ of the whites to the yolk mixture, folding until well blended. Then fold in remaining whites. Add flour and fold in until blended. Blend in butter. Grease the bottoms of 3, 8-inch cake pans and line with wax paper. Divide batter into pans. Bake at 350° for 20-30 minutes, or until toothpick comes out clean. When slightly cooled, remove from pan and cool on racks.

Butter Cream Frosting

1 cup granulated sugar
¾ cup water
3 egg whites
1 cup confectioners' sugar
1½ cups butter
½ cup shortening (Crisco)

In a small saucepan, combine granulated sugar and water. Cook and stir until sugar dissolves, then cover and cook rapidly for 5 minutes. Remove lid and boil until mixture reaches 240° on candy thermometer.

While sugar mixture boils, beat egg whites until stiff. Gradually add the confectioners' sugar. Beat until sugar mixture reaches 240°. Remove sugar water from heat and, in a fine stream, add the syrup to the egg whites, beating constantly. Continue beating until cold.

Beat butter and the shortening until light and creamy. Add to the egg mixture, beating until smooth. Frost the three layers, sides and tops. If frosting gets too soft, refrigerate it and then re-beat.

Nut Brittle

2 cups granulated sugar
1 cup sliced almonds

Put sugar in skillet and melt over medium heat, stirring constantly until sugar is melted and caramel colored. Immediately stir in nuts. Work fast and spread on a well-buttered sheet pan. Cool completely.

Break into pieces and put in a plastic bag to further crush into smaller pieces. Cover the top and sides of the torte. Any leftover brittle can be eaten as candy!

12 servings

Note...
When assembling cake put strips of wax paper around the serving dish so when you are finished frosting and adding the nut brittle, you can pull the wax paper out and your plate will be clean.

Y

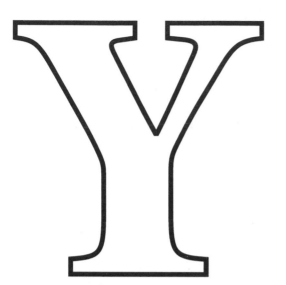

R·e·c·i·p·e·s

When I was 10 my Aunt Lucille served fried pumpkin blossoms. I waited 60 years to try this truly elegant side dish on my own!

Yellow Squash Blossoms

Different varieties of squash or pumpkin blossoms can be used in this recipe. Remember to only pick the male blossoms in the squash patch!

12 blossoms
2 eggs, beaten
2 cups bread crumbs
1 teaspoon salt
½ teaspoon pepper
4 tablespoons butter
2 tablespoons oil

Carefully wash blossoms. Gently fold in half so that the blossom is flat. Dip into beaten eggs, then into the crumbs that were seasoned with salt and pepper. Sauté in butter and oil until lightly browned.

4-6 servings

Note: Herbs could be added to the crumbs.

Yellow Brick Benedict

1 cup butter
4 egg yolks
2 tablespoons lemon juice
¼ teaspoon salt
pinch cayenne
4 slices ham, halved
8 slices Holland Rusk or toast rounds
8 eggs, poached
Hollandaise sauce (recipe follows)

Warm ham, place on top of the rusks. Top with poached eggs. Cover with Hollandaise sauce. Sprinkle with paprika and garnish with parsley.

Heat butter until bubbly. Meanwhile, in blender, put egg yolks, lemon juice, salt and pepper. Cover and blend on high; slowly add butter in a steady stream.

4 servings

Note…
Knorrs packaged Hollandaise can also be used with great success.

Yellow Squash Boats

2 medium yellow summer squash
2 tablespoons olive oil
½ cup chopped onion
1 clove garlic, minced
½ red pepper, chopped
½ cup seeded, chopped tomato
2 tablespoons fresh chopped basil
salt and pepper to taste
4 tablespoons grated, fresh Parmesan cheese

Cut squash in half. Scoop out squash leaving a ¼-inch shell. Cube the scooped-out squash and reserve for filling. In a small amount of water, cook the squash shells or 3 or 4 minutes for just until barely tender. Place upside down on a paper towel to cool.

In the oil, sauté onion, garlic, red pepper and reserved squash until tender. Stir in tomato and basil and cook for 1 minute; add salt and pepper. Fill shells and top with Parmesan cheese. Bake at 350º for 15-20 minutes or until heated through.

4 servings

Note…
A nice accompaniment to beef or pork.

Zinger

Spell it as you wish, ("Aquavit," "Akevitt," or Nell's favorite, "Ahhh-quavit") but for goodness sake don't go through life without sampling the nectar of the norsewomen and norsemen. For many centuries Scandinavians have extolled the life-enhancing qualities of a chilled dose of this heart-warming liqueur distilled from potatoes or grain and flavored with anything from caraway, dill and coriander to cinnamon, purslane and bitter wormwood.

Aquavit stands up to any smoky, salty, rich or creamy foods. Why not warm up a frigid, Wisconsin, winter weekend with Aquavit and pickled fish, smoked salmon or lox and bagels? Feel your taste buds burst as they encounter, crisp roast duck sandwiches, rich liver pate, or succulent roast beef washed down with a hearty Aquavit chaser.

Presenting Aquavit can be great fun! For festivities freeze a bright green bottle of Aquavit in a block of ice garnished with cranberries. A tried and true Scandinavian custom is for the hostess or host of a dinner party to look each guest in the eye as they are being toasted with what else, Aquavit!

Nell's own special Aquavit custom was born at the Painted Lady years ago. After a particularly stressful evening in the kitchen she would retrieve an ice-cold bottle of Aquavit from the fridge, set up several cordial glasses, gather together a few cohorts (usually John Holfeltz and Ken Kohls), look them straight in the eye and – down the hatch.

SKöLL!

Notes...

*I*ndex...

*I*ndex...

Index...